PLANTING
FOR
HONEYBEES

PLANTING
FOR
HONEYBEES

The Grower's Guide
to Creating a Buzz

SARAH WYNDHAM LEWIS

ILLUSTRATED BY JAMES WESTON LEWIS

Hardie Grant

QUADRILLE

DEDICATION

To my mother Evelyn, my Aunt Diana, my Uncle Tod and all the other wonderful gardeners in my family who must have thought I wasn't listening all those years. But somehow, I must have been. A bit.

To my husband, Dale Gibson, for introducing the bees into our life – and somehow sliding it past me that it would take over everything. And for hoping I wouldn't notice that beekeepers can't take summer holidays. (Still grappling with that one…)

To Edward Pug, stalwart canine companion.

CONTENTS

INTRODUCTION

A book of ideas, not a book of instructions

This is not a gardening book. It's a book of information and ideas to enjoy at any level you choose, whether you're an experienced gardener or an absolute beginner.

It's about honeybees and the plants you can grow in your garden to provide them with the pollen and nectar they need. There are about 25,000 different species of bee worldwide, of which only seven species are honeybees, and a lot depends on them. The majority of the plants honeybees pollinate provide food for humans, animals, birds and insects, so planting specifically for them has powerful and direct ecological benefits.

Amongst pollinating insects, honeybees have relatively short tongues. This limits the types of flowers they can access to harvest nectar from. However, planting for honeybees doesn't mean that other pollinators won't benefit. What the honeybees can feed on, so can many bumblebees, hover flies and other important pollinating insects. But not necessarily vice versa.

Although my husband, Dale Gibson, and I run Bermondsey Street Bees together, I leave the hives to Dale. I've had an allergy to insect stings since childhood… and I look rubbish in a beesuit! But I'm fascinated and enchanted by bees and appalled by the complexity and number of threats to their future.

One of my greatest pleasures has been establishing my own garden at our bee yard in Suffolk to observe the preferences and habits of the hives we keep there. It's a perpetual work in progress and I don't spend nearly enough time there, so, coincidentally, it has also evolved to be a very hardy, low-maintenance garden. Which, since I'm not at all a 'grown-up' gardener, is a good thing...

Nevertheless, it has taught me that the most important thing is to get out there and get planting. Wherever, however. Don't get hung up on technicalities. It's perfectly feasible to start from zero and learn as you go along. So if you want to help the honeybee in the most positive way possible, start here.

CHAPTER ONE

WHY THIS BOOK IS NEEDED

After 100 million years on earth, times have never been tougher for the honeybee. Amongst the thousands of types of bee worldwide, it has evolved to be the one on which plants and humans so depend.

Yet despite its importance, the honeybee is assailed by threats on every side, from loss of habitat, use of agrichemicals and climate change to a truly mind-blowing cast of native and foreign bacterial diseases, fungi, parasites and predators, any one of which has the potential to wipe out a colony, sometimes in just a matter of hours.

Globally, the varroa mite (*Varroa destructor*) is named by scientists and beekeepers as the single biggest threat to bees. This blood-sucking parasite pierces the bee's exoskeleton (its protective 'armour'), creating a physical pathway for other diseases to bypass the immune system. Varroa has already decimated wild populations, and the European honeybee (*Apis mellifera*) – the world's most widely managed bee – has not yet evolved to deal with it.

Nowadays, good beekeepers are no longer simply guardians. They must also be stout defenders of their bees, educated and proactive in keeping the hives alive and well without resorting to chemical interventions.

As with any living creature, honeybee health starts with a plentiful and varied diet to give them resilience to external pressures. This highlights the other equally profound crisis facing our bees: loss of food sources.

In many areas of the UK, modern farming practice favours a monoculture approach (huge areas planted with single crops). Such intensive land use, which also often involves the removal of trees and hedgerows, provides erratic forage for rural honeybees and means they go hungry. It's a process that started during the Second World War when domestic food production became paramount and every piece of spare land was turned to cultivation. There has been a massive loss of pollinator forage since then, with studies showing that over 97 per cent of lowland meadows have disappeared, along with woodland, upland heaths and hedgerows. Good farming practice is fighting back by reducing pesticide use, providing dedicated habitats for bees and employing crop rotation, but it's not enough to make up for what has already been lost.

In cities, there's a slightly different problem. Beekeeping has become super-fashionable and government data shows the number of hives continuing to mushroom whilst urban green spaces are shrinking – waste land is snapped up for housing developments, gardens are paved and decked, driveways are tarmacked, all of which reduce the amount of forage available for honeybees. It is horrifying to know that Greater London is losing its green space at a rate equivalent to two and half times the area of Hyde Park every year (source: GIGL. gigl.org.uk).

But let's not despair. All of us can play our part in supporting the honeybee through planting to increase forage variety and availability. It's never been more important and this book will show you how easy it can be to make a difference.

Start to 'think bee' and it's amazing what you'll achieve.

CHAPTER TWO

THE PLANTS, THE BEES AND MANKIND

oneybees evolved millions of years before mankind, as did plants. Flowers evolved alongside the bees and in the race to spread their genes, made themselves ever more attractive to pollinating insects. Bees and plants together weathered everything that time could throw at them until modern humans arrived and began 'improving' nature.

About 100 million years ago (93 million years before the first proto-humans emerged) plants and bees started an elegant coevolution. Their story begins in the Cretaceous period, when dinosaurs were still very much part of the ecology. Some wind-pollinated plants began developing flowers to attract insects, which were much more dependable as pollinators than pollen carried on air currents. Initially, they lured insects by developing petals as landing pads, conspicuous colours and distinctive scents. Later, they evolved to produce nectar, an irresistible sugar-rich meal.

Fossil records from the Cretaceous period show both the earliest flowering plants (known as angiosperms) and a recognisable honeybee (*Melittosphex burmensis*, found in Myanmar in 2006). Perfectly suited to one another, they prospered in their symbiotic relationship and survived the mass extinction of flora and fauna that spelled the end of the giant dinosaurs 65 million years ago.

Along the way, honeybees began clearly differentiating themselves from their wasp ancestors, evolving unique structures such as a honey sac, a second stomach, to collect nectar, and pollen baskets to gather the bounty of nutritious pollen grains. They also began building colonies, storing and managing supplies and evolving the dance languages and labour division that is still seen today.

Amongst the estimated 25,000 species of bee worldwide today, there are only seven species of honeybee. Unique amongst their kind, they overwinter as a colony, living on honey stored in the wax comb. The most successful of all honeybees, *Apis mellifera* ('European Honeybee') evolved from a cavity-nesting bee currently thought to have spread from Asia to Africa between two and three million years ago and then north into Europe. One of mankind's earliest ancestors, *Homo habilis*, first raided wild bee nests in Africa. It was the original luxury food.

Time moved on. The flowers and the bees continued their quiet courtship and eventually, around 12,000 and 11,000 years ago, *Homo sapiens* gradually started to select and breed plants and animals. The clock for a major ecological shift had started ticking. Life was going to change significantly for the honeybee and, it turns out, for flowering plants, too.

Everywhere honeybees were to be found, man harvested honey from wild colonies and then learned how to farm them, first by claiming and tending nests and later by building purpose-designed 'nests' in pots and baskets to attract swarms; these were the earliest hives. By the time of the First Dynasty of Ancient Egypt (c. 3000 BC) hieroglyphs depict bees being kept in mud tubes horizontally stacked to form wall structures.

All over the world, successive cultures have practised beekeeping, and honey and beeswax have provided essential ingredients for everything from food, religious ceremonies and embalming to cosmetics, art and much else. For example, the earliest copper objects cast in the lost-wax process were found in Israel, wrapped in reed mats later carbon dated to between 3500 and 2800 BC.

Ancient Roman rock hives from around 218 BC

The 'WBC' hive, invented by William Broughton Carr in 1890 and still widely used today

While man's relationship with the honeybee has largely been to nurture and protect it, the same cannot be said of flowering plants once mankind began domesticating wild food crops on a larger scale, saving and sowing seed from preferred plants. Transitioning from nomadic hunter gatherers to settled farmers with storerooms allowed humans the leisure to explore their creativity and satisfy their restless curiosity, enabling a life beyond the requirements of simply staying alive.

The artistic eye that saw even our earliest ancestors produce sublime cave paintings and embellished pottery is an innate part of the modern human's skill set, as is our perpetual search for the beautiful and the unique. It was only a matter of time before that eye turned towards the countless species of exquisite wildflowers, still peacefully advertising their wares to the industrious honeybee.

Ancient Egyptian tomb paintings and the remains of flower garlands placed on mummies show that the Egyptians cultivated both native and imported species, including cornflowers, daisies, chrysanthemums, hollyhocks, red poppies, jasmine and roses. Even then, flowers were beginning to be chosen for particular qualities of colour, scent, size and petal formation. Ultimately, making these selections led to an emergence of specific 'garden flowers' in many different places, including the Middle East and China.

Fast forward to Europe in the late 1500s. The development of herbs, fruits, vegetables and garden flowers through importation, selection and deliberate or accidental crossbreeding began to elevate gardening into an art, supported by wealthy patrons. By this time, the simple wild forms of many flowers had become the extreme dandies of the horticultural world. Tulips, long cultivated and refined by the Turks in the Ottoman Empire, were exported to Europe where they were transformed by the Dutch into frilly, virus-streaked, multi-petalled, crazily coloured living artworks. So prized were the plants that they triggered 'Tulipmania', the very first commodity boom (amazingly, in 1633 one bulb of the variety 'Semper Augustus' was valued at about £60,000 in today's currency), which reached its height (and downfall) in early 1637. Many other plant species, including hyacinths, auriculas, and orchids, have spawned similar excitements.

The problem for the honeybee is that plants continue to be bred like this, rapidly moving away from the time-crafted architecture of the ancient wildflower forms. We are offered ever-brighter/-bigger/-smaller/-hardier/-earlier/-later flowering forms, with more novel or more complex petal structures, usually at the cost of accessible pollen and nectar. Many are sterile. As a consequence, today's gardens full of beautiful ornamental flowers might offer little sustenance to honeybees or the many other pollinators who evolved slowly alongside the wild forms. Compare a showy pompom dahlia with its densely clustered and folded petals to the delicious pollen-packed open flower-head of its earlier type, which looks exactly like what it is – a giant daisy.

This is why there is so much noise nowadays around growing wildflowers. But please don't get hung up on this. Wildflowers are very important, *but they are not definitive* in honeybee plantings. As you read this book, you'll see that careful choices of plants, often favouring older, wilder varieties, give you a virtually limitless range of honeybee-friendly plants for every situation, from the smallest to the largest, most formal garden. The pact between plants, bees and mankind can still be kept.

CHAPTER THREE

TEN IMPORTANT THINGS TO KNOW

about planting
for honeybees

I f you read nothing else in this whole book, please read this chapter. Armed with these guiding principles, you'll be able not only to plan your own space, but also to impress friends with brief but impressively knowledgeable lectures on how to plant specifically for honeybees!

QUANTITY, QUALITY AND VARIETY

Plentiful supplies of varied forage are essential to help honeybees withstand the impact of disease and harmful environmental factors. In a single foraging trip, a honeybee will visit around 100 flowers, and she (all worker bees are female) will make around 10 to 15 trips in a day. So that's at least 1,000 flowers a day, and this is a conservative estimate – it's said that a honeybee might visit up to 5,000 flowers on a productive day.

FOUR-SEASON PLANTING

Although March to September are the key months for honeybees, they will fly whenever the temperature is above 10°C (50°F), even in the depths of winter. So early- and late-flowering plants are especially valuable. Ideally, plant 'sequentially' so that there is always something in flower.

MOW LESS AND LOVE WEEDS

Many so-called lawn 'weeds' provide precious forage. Mow lawns but less often and leave some areas to grow wilder. This encourages useful species to grow, such as daisies, trefoil, clovers and especially dandelions, which are vitally important as an early season nectar source.

BEES SEE BLUE

The photoreceptors in honeybees' eyes see from yellow, blue and green right up into the ultraviolet (UV) light scale. This makes blue, violet, purple and white flowers especially attractive to them. They can also distinguish orange blooms, but the colour red looks black to a bee, making red flowers unappealing. Some flowers exploit UV light to alert bees. The outer edges of the petals reflect UV light, while the nectar-rich centres absorb it to present a dark patch (rather like a bull's eye), signaling the perfect landing pad.

'FLOWER FIDELITY'

Honeybees only visit one type of flower in any one foraging trip. This is called 'flower fidelity' and is what makes them such effective pollinators. By planting large clumps or 'drifts' of single species you can save the bees' energy and optimise each of their trips.

NATIVE AND NON-NATIVE

Honeybees have evolved alongside certain flower species in every region. The flowers, too, are perfectly attuned to that region. For these reasons, some people favour using only native plantings in their gardens. However, widespread climate change means that many non-native species have now become very valuable additions to our pollinator forage and are widely accepted by honeybees as part of a changing flora.

TEN IMPORTANT THINGS TO KNOW...

THINK BUSHES AND TREES

Bees are naturally tree dwellers and feeders and, if space allows, bee-friendly plantings should always start with a framework of durable, perennial forage from bushes and trees. A single lime (linden) tree in flower provides the same amount of forage as 3000 sq m (32,292 sq ft) of wildflower meadow (which is about half the size of a football pitch)!

 ## KEEP IT SIMPLE

With shorter tongues than bumblebees or butterflies, honeybees often can't feed from complex flower structures. Showy, highly bred ornamental flowers often give little or no forage. Generally, stay close to the original wild or simpler forms of flowers where nectar and pollen are easily accessible.

 ## WATER, WATER

Bees don't store water in the hive. They forage for it as needed and they often choose surprising sources. If you don't have a pond, a bowl of pebbles full of rainwater provides a good stop off. In hot weather, water brought back by forager bees is sprinkled over the brood cells (nests) and then fanned by worker bees to cool the area through evaporation. Honey stored in the hive is diluted before being eaten, so water gathering is often the reason for bees flying on warm winter days.

GARDEN ORGANICALLY

Read up on organic gardening techniques. There are many wildlife-friendly alternatives, but if you absolutely must use chemicals, follow the manufacturer's instructions carefully to prevent overdosing. As far as is possible, source your seeds, plants bulbs and potting compost from organic nurseries, this will ensure that they have never been treated with insecticides.

CHAPTER FOUR

READING
THE
LABEL

This chapter is the only one that is just for beginners. Throughout this book, I've kept everything as straightforward as possible because I want to encourage people just to start planting, and not be worried by too much detail. But there are a few simple concepts that, if you want to make a success of your plantings, can really make a difference. Essentially, the more you know about your plot and the plants you have in mind, the better the choices you can make. It's all about reading the label.

SUNNY OR SHADY?

The majority of plants are quite picky about their location. Some will only thrive in full sun, others prefer (or will tolerate) partial shade, and there are plants that will grow in deep shade. Full sun means that a plant requires at least six hours of direct sun a day; partial shade indicates that a plant needs three to six hours of direct sun a day; and deep-shade plants will grow with less than two hours of direct sun a day.

Ideally, honeybees prefer to forage in the sun. This is for two reasons. The first is that (unlike bumblebees, which have very furry bodies) they are susceptible to chill. The second reason is that nectar flow is greatly increased by warmth and sunlight, making plants in sunny positions their best bet for foraging.

It's worth observing where you are planning to plant and mapping out your sunny and shady patches. Some areas of the garden may be sunny all day, others only part of the day – but it's good to know so that you can choose plants accordingly. Whether you are searching online or in a garden centre, you will find plants are usually sold with information about their preferred location (if not, you'll easily be able to look it up).

HOW BIG?

Another fundamental piece of information you need to know about any plant is its ultimate size. Again check the labelling or plant description online. You need to know both how tall it will grow and also how wide, i.e. how much elbow room it's going to need, and how many years it will take to reach maximum growth. Most plants don't like being squashed in and you can only prune to a certain extent – so if something you want to plant is going to outgrow the space available, look for another version of it. There are usually smaller/dwarf cultivars available.

GARDEN THUGS

Some of the plants listed in this book are wild at heart and would like nothing better than to take over a garden, either via a vigorous root system (e.g. comfrey and mint) or by self-seeding (e.g. poppies). This may not matter if you have a large space, but in a small garden you may need to tame the enthusiasts by planting invasive species in pots (which you can then sink into a flowerbed) or removing seed heads before they mature. A little research will tell you more about the spreading tendencies of any plant.

SOIL TYPE?

If you are planting in containers, soil type is not usually an issue. But where you are planting into beds it is a great help to know what sort of soil you have. There are many different types, from free-draining sandy soils to dense, claggy clays and much in between. The Royal Horticultural Society (rhs.org.uk) has an excellent online guide to soil types to help you identify what sort of soil you have and how to make the most of it. Understanding soil types is not complicated and it will help you be much more successful with your plantings.

You also need to know the chemistry of your soil (soil pH), i.e. whether it is acid or alkaline. Different plants have evolved to thrive in different pH levels, for instance heathers flourish in acid soils, while hebes do well in alkaline soils. A DIY soil testing kit, available from garden centres or to order online, will tell you whether your garden soil is acidic or alkaline.

If the soil doesn't suit them, you will lose plants or you will spend a lot of time digging in other materials to try to improve the soil and make them happier. Far better to know a bit about your soil and choose plants likely to thrive in it.

KNOW YOUR PLANTS

Some plants come back year after year. Some don't. Some lose their leaves all at once, others don't. Some overwinter without fuss, whilst others need cosseting. Here is a very short glossary to help you understand the terms used to describe these differences.

ANNUAL

Lasting only one year before dying away, annuals often have profuse blooms and bring instant glamour to the garden. Some annuals self-seed and will grow back from seed year after year. Annuals often have good pollen and nectar to offer honeybees, but tend to flower from midsummer onwards, contributing little to early forage availability.

PERENNIAL

The mainstay of most plantings, perennial plants carry on growing from year to year. Gardeners refer to any long-lived plant that's not a tree, shrub, climber or bulb as a perennial. They often flower early in the season, bringing much-needed forage to honeybees as they build up their colony numbers in spring. Perennials can be deciduous (herbaceous perennials that die down completely in the autumn) or evergreen (see below).

Ideally, use perennials to create the structure of your plantings and then add annuals for even more colour and interest. This supplies multi-season forage.

DECIDUOUS

Trees, shrubs, climbers and perennials that are deciduous lose all of their leaves at some point in the year. In temperate climates, this is usually in the autumn.

EVERGREEN

As their name suggests, evergreen trees, shrubs, climbers and perennials shed and grow leaves continuously so that they appear green all year round.

HARDY

The hardiness of a plant refers to its ability to survive tough weather conditions. A hardy plant will withstand a cold winter, including hard frosts, and weather extremes without needing special care. Hardiness is graded, so that you may find terms such as 'half hardy' or 'tender' (i.e. not at all hardy!) used to describe plants you are looking at. Unless you live in a warm microclimate, it's simpler for beginners to choose hardier plants at first.

FLOWERING SEASONS

The exact time when plants flower can vary by several weeks, depending on your local climate. For general reference though, horticulturalists define the flowering seasons in the Northern Hemisphere as:-

SPRING: March, April, May

SUMMER: June, July, August

AUTUMN: September, October, November

WINTER: December, January, February

r: Peony

CHAPTER FIVE

OF NECTAR, POLLEN AND PROPOLIS

Honeybees gather three key substances from plants: nectar, pollen and resin. The honeybee is both a pragmatist and an alchemist and transforms what it gathers into unique and extraordinary substances. These serve the hive's every need and have also been widely used by humans for centuries.

NECTAR (HONEY)

A rich sugary substance secreted by plant glands called nectaries, nectar is the raw material for honey. This is a vital source of food for the bee and contains carbohydrates and many other nutritional elements, including vitamins, lipids, volatile essential oils and minerals. When a forager bee visits nectar-bearing plants (which are far rarer than plants that produce pollen) she uses her proboscis as a drinking straw to suck the nectar into a special honey storage stomach. Within the nectar sac, enzymes from the bee's saliva begin to break down the complex sugars (sucrose) into simple sugars (glucose and fructose), in a process known as inversion. Having visited 100 or more flowers, she returns to the hive. Waiting for her are receiver house bees. The forager bee passes the nectar to them mouth-to-mouth in a system called trophallaxis. Each receiver bee then continues the inversion process inside its own honey sac.

What many people don't know, though, is that bees are not fussy about where they find their sugars. Tree aphids produce honeydew, a sugar-rich secretion that bees gather from the leaves and turn into honey. Dark, pungent and gelatinous, this is hugely prized in many countries. Equally, any drop of spilled honey will be swiftly reclaimed, and I have even seen our

Suffolk bees beating the wasps to feast on windfall plums at the end of the summer.

Nectar brought into the hive may contain up to 80 per cent water. To prevent fermentation and create their honey stores, receiver bees set to work to evaporate off most of the water content. Bringing a drop of nectar up from their honey sacs, they roll it in their mouths so that the nectar is exposed to the air to dry. More drops of nectar are added until the drop is the right size and consistency to be deposited in a honeycomb cell. Finally, they fan their wings to evaporate further excess water from the cells, taking the moisture level down to 17 per cent. The sound of thousands of bees' wings acting as a giant fan is the source of the 'hum' we hear from a busy summer hive. Finally, they seal the cell with a beeswax capping. Safe from air and water, the honey inside will last indefinitely.

Adult bees feed on nectar, both out in the field and during the exchange process, but in winter or other times of need, the stored honey will be uncapped and mixed with water before being consumed in the hive. Diluted honey is also used, along with nectar and pollen, to feed young larvae. Good beekeepers never remove the honey stores needed to keep colonies alive and well during lean months (at least 20kg/40lb per hive). Fortunately, honeybees often produce more honey than they need, especially if they are given sufficient space to store it. Out of respect for the bees and as a matter of sustainability, only that excess honey should ever be taken from the hive.

The very first form of sweetness accessible to mankind, honey in its natural 'raw' form verges on the miraculous. It is packed with nutrients, including amino acids (proteins), vitamins B, A, C, D, E and K, and a range of minerals and trace elements.

Honey has always been esteemed for its healing properties and modern medicine is beginning to catch up with older wisdom, making honey the subject of ongoing research in several areas. Manuka has been widely promoted as 'the' medical honey, but wider analysis now shows almost every unprocessed honey has its own unique properties, including antibacterial, antiviral, antioxidant, antifungal and anti-inflammatory properties.

Unfortunately, the very properties that make honey so delicious and so valuable also lead to it being commoditised. Said to be

Honeybees appreciate single petalled, open flower forms

one of the most widely adulterated foodstuffs on earth (other well-known degraded foods include olive oil, spices and wine), it suffers from exploitative production processes and widespread commercial treatments, which destroy much of its nutritional value and active constituents. This includes blending honey from many sources; bulking out with cheap sweeteners such as corn syrup; pasteurising, which damages precious enzymes and amino acids; and micro-filtration, which removes nutritionally important pollens because they cause 'commercially undesirable' crystallisation. Filtering out pollens also removes the DNA of the honey, making its true origins impossible to trace. Buying raw honey from trusted sources will always be the best way to ensure that you get the real thing.

POLLEN

Most plants reproduce by pollination, which is the transfer of pollen (male sex cells produced in the male part of the flower) to the stigma (the female part of the flower). The hairy honeybee seeking food unwittingly captures and transfers the powdery pollen grains between plants of the same species to achieve effective cross-pollination.

Honeybees collect pollen as a food for the hive. Being vegetarian, bees depend on pollen as their only source of protein. It also contains lipids, minerals, vitamins, amino acids and many other key nutrients. Adult bees need very little protein, so its main use is in feeding the brood and newly hatched bees.

Foraging bees visit pollen-bearing plants, stuffing the grains into the 'baskets' on their back legs. Beekeepers can tell precisely what their bees are feeding on by the colour of the incoming pollen on the bees' legs. The pollens from individual plants vary widely in both their colour and their nutritional profile, so it's important for honeybees to access a wide variety of plants to achieve a balanced diet.

Back at the hive, house bees help to empty foragers' baskets and store the pollen in the cells of the comb. The bees headbutt the grains into the cells in order to pack in as much of the precious resource as possible, usually close to the brood cells (these house eggs, larvae and pupae). The nurse bees who tend the brood depend on pollen to produce royal jelly, a protein-rich, gelatinous, white substance secreted from glands on their heads. This is used to feed both very young drone and worker larvae for a short period of time, and to create and develop queen bees.

Relatively little pollen is stored in the hive at any one time, so bees need access to pollen-bearing flowers, trees and bushes for as much of the year as possible.

A small amount of pollen can safely be taken from the hive occasionally, using pollen traps to brush just a few grains off the

Pollen mound

legs of incoming foragers. Many people swear by taking local pollen as a remedy for hay fever. It has culinary uses too; chefs and bartenders like the burst of floral aromas in fresh pollen. As pollen ages, it gains a deeper, mustier flavour profile.

RESIN (PROPOLIS)

One of the more extraordinary substances to come from the beehive is propolis. Prized for centuries as a medicinal substance and a base component of incense and other perfumes, it is gathered by honeybees in the form of resins from tree buds, sap flows and other sources. It has a distinctive, woody, resinous fragrance.

Mixed with bee saliva, pollen and beeswax, the resins become propolis, the single most versatile substance produced by bees. It is used as a building material to stop up small gaps in the hive, increase its stability and reduce vibrations. Highly antimicrobial, antibacterial and antifungal, it is also part of the hive's defence against disease, especially from incoming fungal spores or bacteria. Additionally, bees will also use it to 'mummify' small creatures, such as mice, which have got into the hive and been stung to death as intruders but are too big for the bees to remove. Sealing the carcass in a propolis shroud prevents the disease potential of it rotting in the hive. Some species of wild bees even use propolis to build a firewall, giving their nest some protection from forest fires.

With its unique array of medicinal properties, propolis has been used by mankind for thousands of years and is still the subject of much research into potential new drugs.

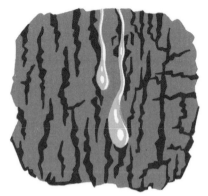

Resin, seeping out of tree bark

BEESWAX

Making beeswax is a costly investment for honeybees, requiring the energy from around 3kg (7lb) of honey consumed to produce just 450g (1lb) of precious wax.

The primary building material of the hive, beeswax is an extraordinary substance produced exclusively by young bees. Special glands on their abdomens convert honey into a wax that is exuded as tiny translucent flakes to be gathered by older bees. They will then chew it, a process that makes the wax more malleable. Once ready, it is used to build comb, one of the natural world's most extraordinary feats of geometric precision that also, miraculously, uses the least amount of precious beeswax. Bees maintain the brood nest at a temperature between 32°C and 35°C (90°F and 95°F), which is also the ideal temperature for them to work the wax.

The bees work together to 'draw out' the comb, building the deep hexagonal (six-sided) cells slightly canted upwards to hold liquid honey. The completed comb defines the hive. It is a nursery, a storeroom, a dance floor and a stage for the complex life of the colony. The first thing a swarm of bees will do when it finds a new home is to build comb.

Beeswax is an invaluable substance for humans too, used for countless purposes over the centuries. Ancient cultures depended on it to maintain their wigs, moisturise their skin, create writing tablets, preserve papyrus documents and embalm their dead. Medieval monks cherished it as a clean-burning alternative to animal fat candles and documented its healing properties in salves and balms. Historically – and still today – it's a vital ingredient in many industrial and artisanal processes including food production (e.g. for coating cheeses), cosmetics, metal castings, medicines, glues, engraving, textiles and much, much more.

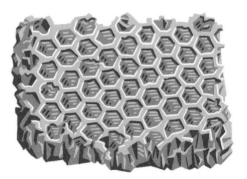

Wax drawn out by bees to create comb

CHAPTER SIX

PLANTING
RECOMMENDATIONS

E ach plant recommendation is listed in the season in which it is well known for flowering. However, you will find that many species flower across a couple of seasons and that you can often buy early- or late-flowering varieties, some of which are also included in the lists below.

Equally, you'll find some plants are listed in several sections. That's either because they come in many sizes or because they are just so brilliant for bees and we should all plant them as widely as possible.

In the interest of getting started with the concept of bee-friendly plantings, plants are listed using the names they're most commonly referred to (in some instances, this may be the same as their Latin name). So, for example, where 'sunflower' is recommended, experienced gardeners or those with enquiring minds can use that as a launch pad to explore the many sunflower varieties available. Masses of advice and information is available online, in gardening books and from staff at garden centres and nurseries. Be aware, though, that many modern, highly cultivated plants may have little to offer honeybees in the way of nectar, so qualify your research with the term 'bee-friendly'.

If you don't want to do any research, just use the 'Ten of the Best' listings in Chapter Seven (see pages 103–107) as an introduction to planting for honeybees and take it from there.

HOW TO USE THIS SECTION

If you've only got a tiny garden space, it's really not a lot of use to be given a list of bee-friendly shrubs. The following lists are organised on the basis that most of us start thinking about gardening from the space available to us, be that a modest windowsill or rolling acres.

Find the closest description to the space you have available and start from there. In each category, plants are suggested that are size appropriate and rewarding to grow. If you want recommendations for larger or smaller plantings, just look in the appropriate sections.

HOW THE PLANTS WERE CHOSEN

They say that if you have four beekeepers in a room, you'll have six opinions on any given topic! I've never found this truer than in researching this book. From both expert and amateur sources, the recommendations and opinions on bee-friendly plants differ wildly.

My research, therefore, covered the widest possible range of sources available to me, from beekeepers' and gardeners' verbal and recorded observations, bee sightings posted on social media and scientific studies, wildflower lore and the wisdom of traditional nursery growers. I know from my own gardening experiences in London and Suffolk that the bees will sometimes disdain so-called 'bee magnet' plants to feast on something so small and humble that I've virtually overlooked it.

The simple answer is, if the bees like it – plant more. If you never ever see a single pollinating insect, let alone a honeybee, on a particular plant, you have nothing to lose by trying something else in that location.

P.S. Remember to try and source organic plants, bulbs, seeds and composts that have not been pre-treated with insecticides.

WINDOWSILLS AND SMALL BALCONIES

Even if all you have is a narrow window ledge or a tiny balcony, there is still a good choice of plants you can grow for the bees.

Herbs are ideal for small-scale gardening, but will only benefit pollinators if you let them flower. Generally, gardeners recommend pinching out the tops of herbs to prevent them flowering and optimise flavour. Solve this by letting some flower and keeping others for the kitchen.

There are plenty of other options listed here, too, giving year-round interest and honeybee forage.

SPRING

 FLOWERS: Alpine Aster, Aubrieta, Coltsfoot, Cowslip, Crocus, Delosperma, Dwarf Hebe, Forget-me-not, Grape Hyacinth, Heather, Hellebore, Hyacinth, Pasque Flower, Potentilla, Sea Pink, Star of Bethlehem, Sweet Pea, Wallflower, Wood Anemone

 EDIBLES: Chervil, Chive, Rosemary, Strawberry

SUMMER

 FLOWERS: Alpine Aster, Alyssum, Aster/
Michaelmas Daisy, Gypsophila, Black-Eyed Susan,
Clover, Cornflower, Delosperma, Dwarf Godetia,
Dwarf Hebe, Dwarf Veronica/Speedwell, Forget-
me-not, Heather, Potentilla, Scabious, Sea Pink,
Serbian Bellflower, Stonecrop, Sweet Pea, Wallflower

 EDIBLES: Autumn Sage, Basil, Chervil,
Chive, Dwarf Lavender, Lemon Verbena, Mint,
Nasturtium, Oregano, Pot Marigold, Rosemary,
Sage, Strawberry, Sweet Marjoram, Thyme

l: Forget-me-not
r: Aster

AUTUMN

 FLOWERS: Aster/Michaelmas Daisy, Autumn Crocus, Autumn Hawkbit, Autumn Stonecrop, Black-Eyed Susan, Cyclamen, Delosperma, Dwarf Godetia, dwarf Hebe, Dwarf Veronica/Speedwell, Heather, Scabious

 EDIBLES: Autumn Sage, Nasturtium, Oregano, Pot Marigold, Rosemary, Sweet Marjoram

WINTER
INTO SPRING

Winter is a lean time and there are far fewer plant choices, especially for small-scale plantings. The answer is to plant masses of the same type of plant together: these very late/very early flowers look really decorative in dense clumps. And grouping by species also makes foraging easier for honeybees when they venture out on warmer days.

 FLOWERS: Cyclamen, Heather, Hellebore Rock Cress, Snowdrop, Sweet Violet, Wallflower, Winter Aconite, Winter Crocus, Winter Pansy

l: Winter Pansy
r: Snowdrop

PATIOS, DECKS AND TERRACES

Even the smallest patio, deck or terrace offers so many different planting opportunities – from tubs brimming with herbs, flowers or small bushes to profusely flowering climbers supported on walls or trellis. You could even create a 'living wall' or grow vegetables in pots (see pages 83 and 87).

One of the pleasures of planting in containers is that you can group and re-group them to find the ideal situation for your plants or style your outdoor space. And because you are not planting directly into existing earth, you can tailor the soil mix and feed for specific plants if they need extra encouragement.

SPRING

 FLOWERS: Allium, Aubrieta, Coltsfoot, Cowslip, Cranesbill/Hardy Geranium, Crocus, Deadnettle, Delosperma, Forget-me-not, Grape Hyacinth, Hellebore, Hyacinth, Leopards's Bane, Pasque Flower, Poppy, Sea Pink, Sweet Pea, Wallflower, Wood Anemone

 CLIMBERS: Clematis, Wisteria

 COMPACT BUSHES: Berberis, Box, compact Hebe, Heather, Mahonia, Mexican Orange, Potentilla, Skimmia

 EDIBLES: Borage, Chervil, Chive, Rosemary, Strawberry

A NOTE ON GROWING CLIMBERS IN POTS: climbing plants need root space, so choose the largest feasible container and maybe a compact version of the plant. If you have room to build raised beds, they will improve life for both bushes and the bigger, more ambitious climbers such as roses and hydrangeas.

SUMMER

 FLOWERS: Agastache, Allium, Alyssum, Arnica, Aster/Michalmas Daisy, Bee Balm, Catmint, Catnip, Common Fleabane, Common Knapweed, Cornflower, Cosmos, Cranesbill/Hardy Geranium, Deadnettle, Delosperma, Dwarf Godetia, Fiddleneck, Flax, Forget-me-not, Germander, Helenium, Mexican Fleabane, Ox-Eye Daisy, Poppy, Purple Viper's Bugloss, Scabious, Sea Pink, Stonecrop, Sweet Mignonette, Sweet William, Sweet Pea, Verbena, Veronica/Speedwell, Viper's Bugloss, Wallflower, Yarrow

 CLIMBERS: Black-Eyed Susan Vine, Climbing Hydrangea, Climbing and Rambling Roses, Passion Flower, Tufted Vetch, Virginia Creeper

 COMPACT BUSHES: compact Buddleja, compact Hebe, Cotoneaster, Feverfew, Heather, Potentilla, Rock Rose, small Abelias, Tree/Shrubby Germander

 EDIBLES: Autumn Sage, Basil, Beans, Borage, Chervil, Chive, Courgette, Fennel, Hyssop, Lavender, Lemon Verbena, Mint, Nasturtium, Oregano, Pot Marigold, Rosemary, Sage, Strawberry, Sweet Marjoram, Thyme

l: Sweet William
r: Passion Flower

AUTUMN

 FLOWERS: Agastache, Autumn Crocus, Aster/
Michaelmas Daisy, Autumn Hawkbit, Autumn Ox-
Eye Daisy, Autumn Stonecrop, Black-Eyed Susan,
Bugbane, Catmint, Catnip, Common Fleabane,
Cosmos, Cranesbill/Hardy Geranium, Cyclamen,
Deadnettle, Delosperma, Dwarf Godetia,
Fiddleneck, Germander, Helenium, Japanese
Anemone (smaller varieties), Liatris, Mexican
Fleabane, Poppy, Purple Viper's Bugloss, Scabious,
Sweet Mignonette, Verbena, Yarrow

 CLIMBERS: Autumn Clematis,
Black-Eyed Susan Vine, Common
Ivy, Passion Flower

COMPACT BUSHES:
Bluebeard, compact Buddleja,
compact Hebe, Feverfew,
Heather, Mexican Orange,
small Abelias

 EDIBLES: Autumn Sage, Borage,
Fennel, Hyssop, Nasturtium, Oregano,
Pot Marigold, Rosemary, Sweet Marjoram

WINTER INTO SPRING

 FLOWERS: Cyclamen, Hellebore, Rock Cress, Siberian Squill, Snowdrop, Sweet Violet, Wallflower, Winter Aconite, Winter Crocus, Winter Pansy

 CLIMBERS: Clematis, Vine Lilac, Winter Jasmine

 COMPACT BUSHES: Heather, Mahonia, Winter Daphne, Winter Honeysuckle, Witch Hazel

l: Japanese Anemone
r: Ox-Eye Daisy

SMALL GARDENS

Small gardens can easily produce a bee-thrilling variety of year-round pollen and nectar-bearing flowers, bushy plants and small trees. Keep close-mown lawn to a minimum, pack your beds with plants and position pots on hard-landscaped areas such as terraces or decks. Smother the walls with flowering climbers.

SPRING

 FLOWERS: Allium, Astilbe, Aubretia, Candytuft,
Coltsfoot, Cranesbill/Hardy Geraniums, Crocus,
Deadnettle, Delosperma, Euphorbia, Hellebore,
Hyacinth, Leopard's Bane, Pasque Flower,
Poppy, Solomon's Seal, Sweet Pea, Wallflower,
Wood Anemone

 CLIMBERS: Clematis, Wisteria

 BUSHES AND COMPACT TREES: Berberis,
Box, Ceanothus, Compact Viburnum, Deutzia,
Hawthorn, Heather, Hebe, Goat (Pussy) Willow,
Judas Tree, Mahonia, Mexican Orange,
Potentilla, Skimmia

 EDIBLES: Apple, Borage,
Bramble, Chervil, Chive,
Crab Apple, fruiting Currant,
Quince, Rosemary

SUMMER

 FLOWERS: Allium, Alyssum, Arnica, Aster/Michaelmas Daisy, Astilbe, Astrantia, Baby Blue Eyes, Bee Balm, Black-Eyed Susan, Candytuft, Catmint, Catnip, Coreopsis, Cornflower, Cosmos, Cranesbill/Hardy Geranium, Deadnettle, Delosperma, Euphorbia, Fiddleneck, Flax, Globe Thistle, Goldenrod, Helenium, Heuchera, Hollyhock, Jacob's Ladder, Ox-Eye Daisy, Peony, Phlox, Poppy, Purple Coneflower, Purple Viper's Bugloss, Russian Sage, Salvia, Scabious, Serbian Bellflower, Sweet Mignonette, Sweet Pea, Sweet William, Tobacco Plant, Veronica/Speedwell, Viper's Bugloss, Wallflower, Wood Sage, Yarrow, Zinnia

 CLIMBERS: Black-Eyed Susan Vine, climbing Hydrangea, climbing and rambling Roses, Passion Flower, Tufted Vetch, Virginia Creeper

 BUSHES AND COMPACT TREES:
Buddleja, Ceanothus, compact Viburnum,
Deutzia, Dog Rose, Escallonia, Feverfew,
Golden Rain Tree, Heather, Hebe, Mallow,
Mock Orange, Potentilla, Pyracantha,
Rock Rose, Rose, small Abelias, St. John's Wort

EDIBLES: Autumn Sage, Basil, Beans,
Borage, Bramble, Chervil, Chive,
Courgette, Dill, Fennel, Hyssop, Lavender,
Lemon Verbena, Mint, Nasturtium,
Oregano, Pot Marigold, Rosemary,
Sage, Strawberry, Sweet Marjoram, Thyme

l: Allium
r: Borage

AUTUMN

 FLOWERS: Aster/Michaelmas Daisy, Autumn Ox-Eye Daisy, Autumn Stonecrop, Baby Blue Eyes, Black-Eyed Susan, Bugbane, Catmint, Catnip, Cosmos, Cranesbill/Hardy Geranium, Cyclamen, Deadnettle, Delosperma, Fiddleneck, Goldenrod, Helenium, Japanese Amenone, Liatris, Poppy, Purple Coneflower, Purple Viper's Bugloss, Russian Sage, Scabious, Sweet Mignonette, Tobacco Plant, Veronica/Speedwell, Yarrow, Zinnia

 CLIMBERS: Autumn Clematis, Black-Eyed Susan Vine, Common Ivy, Passion Flower

 BUSHES AND COMPACT TREES: Bluebeard, Buddleja, Ceanothus, Escallonia, Feverfew, Heather, Hebe, Mallow, Mexican Orange, small Abelias, St. John's Wort

 EDIBLES: Autumn Sage, Borage, Fennel, Hyssop, Nasturtium, Oregano, Pot Marigold, Rosemary, Sweet Marjoram

WINTER
INTO SPRING

 FLOWERS: Cyclamen, Hellebore, Rock Cress,
Siberian Squill, Snowdrop, Sweet Violet, Wallflower,
Winter Aconite, Winter Crocus, Winter Hazel

 CLIMBERS: Clematis, Vine Lilac,
Winter Jasmine

 BUSHES AND COMPACT TREES:
Compact Viburnum, Forsythia, Hazel, Heather,
Mahonia, Stachyurus, Sweet Box, Winter
Honeysuckle, Winter Daphne, Winter-
Flowering Cherry, Witch Hazel

l: Helenium
r: Witch Hazel

LARGE GARDENS

Large gardens offer the chance to create the broad swathes of single species planting that honeybees adore. Bushes can be larger species or planted as hedges. Fruiting hedges (with species such as dog rose, blackthorn and blackberry) offer a feast for bees and also provide valuable habitats and food for other insects, birds and small mammals.

Large flowering trees offer magnificent forage and can be underplanted with productive flowers. Grassy margins or open areas can be planted with a profusion of wild flowers. For more flowers, especially more compact ones to work well at the front of borders, look through the planting recommendations in previous sections.

Because of the nature of large gardens, which often have a distinct kitchen garden space, I have not separated edibles in this section. You'll find more in the 'Edible Garden' section (see pages 87–89).

SPRING

 FLOWERS: Allium, Aquilegia, Bleeding Heart, Borage, Bugle, Candytuft, Comfrey, Cranesbill/Hardy Geranium, Crocus, Delosperma, English Bluebell, Euphorbia, Hellebore, Honesty, Hyacinth, Pasque Flower, Poppy, Wallflower

 CLIMBERS: Clematis, Wisteria

 BUSHES: Broom, Ceanothus, Deutzia, flowering Currant, flowering Holly, Gorse, Heather, Hebe, Japanese Quince, Kolkwitzia, Lilac, Lily of the Valley Bush, Mahonia, Mexican Orange, Potentilla, Skimmia, Tree Peony, Viburnum

 TREES: Almond, Blackthorn, Cherry, Elderflower, False Acacia, Goat (Pussy) Willow, Hawthorn, Horse Chestnut, Lilac, Maple, Medlar, Mountain Ash, Oak, Plum, Quince, Sycamore, Whitebeam

SUMMER

 FLOWERS: Allium, Angelica, Aquilegia, Aster/Michaelmas Daisy, Autumn Sage, Bee Balm, Black-Eyed Susan, Blanket Flower, Borage, Bugle, Candytuft, Catmint, Catnip, Comfrey, Common Knapweed, Coreopsis, Cosmos, Cranesbill/Hardy Geraniums, Culver's Root, Dahlia (simple, open-centred varieties), Delosperma, Elecampane, Euphorbia, Evening Primrose, False Indigo, Garden Anchusa/Italian Bugloss, Globe Thistle, Goldenrod, Helenium, Hollyhock, Joe Pye Weed, Lupin, Marsh Mallow, Motherwort, Mullein, Ox-Eye Daisy, Peony, Phlox, Poppy, Purple Coneflower, Rosebay Willowherb, Russian Sage, Salvia, Scabious, Selfheal, Shasta Daisy, Sweet William, Sunflower, Verbena, Viper's Bugloss, White Horehound, Wood Germander, Yarrow, Zinnia

 CLIMBERS: Black-Eyed Susan Vine, Climbing Hydrangea, climbing Nasturtium, climbing and rambling Roses, Passion Flower, Russian Vine, Tufted Vetch, Virginia Creeper

 BUSHES: Abelia, Callicarpa, Ceanothus, Cotoneaster, Deutzia, Dog Rose, Escallonia, Heather, Hebe, Hoheria, Japanese Rose, Kolkwitzia, Lacecap Hydrangea, Mallow, Myrtle, Potentilla, Pyracantha, Snowberry, St. John's Wort, Sweet Olive, Tree Peony, Tree/Shrubby Germander, Viburnum, Weigela

 TREES: Bee Bee Tree (Evodia), Elderflower, Eucalyptus, Eucryphia, False Acacia, Indian Bean Tree, Japanese Angelica, Japanese Pagoda Tree, Lime (Linden), Sumach, Tulip Tree

l: Clematis
r: Peony

AUTUMN

 FLOWERS: Aster/Michaelmas Daisy, Autumn Ox-Eye Daisy, Autumn Sage, Autumn Stonecrop, Black-Eyed Susan, Blanket Flower, Borage, Bugbane, Catmint, Catnip, Common Tansy, Cosmos, Dahlia (simple, open-centred varieties), Delosperma, Evening Primrose, Garden Anchusa/Italian Bugloss, Goldenrod, Helenium, Japanese Anemone, Joe Pye Weed, Marsh Mallow, Phlox, Poppy, Purple Coneflower, Purple Viper's Bugloss, Rosebay Willowherb, Russian Sage, Scabious, Selfheal, Verbena, White Horehound, Yarrow, Zinnia

 CLIMBERS: Autumn Clematis, Black-Eyed Susan Vine, climbing Nasturtium, Common Ivy, Passion Flower, Russian Vine

 BUSHES: Abelia, Bluebeard, Ceanothus, Escallonia, Heather, Hebe, Japanese Aralia, Japanese Rose, Mexican Orange, Snowberry, St. John's Wort, Sweet Olive

TREES: Bee Bee Tree (Evodia), Eucalyptus, Eucryphia, Japanese Angelica, Japanese Pagoda Tree

WINTER INTO SPRING

 FLOWERS: Cyclamen, Heather, Hellebore, Rock Cress, Snowdrop, Sweet Violet, Wallflower, Winter Aconite, Winter Crocus

 CLIMBERS: Clematis, Vine Lilac, Winter Jasmine

 BUSHES: Bodnant Viburnum, Forsythia, Gorse, Heather, Mahonia, Stachyurus, Sweet Box, Viburnum, Winter Daphne, Winter Honeysuckle, Witch Hazel

 TREES: Alder, Hazel, Willow, Winter-Flowering Cherry

l: Japanese Aralia
r: Pussy Willow

MARSHY PLANTS

If there's a boggy patch in your garden, or pond margins that you would like to plant for honeybees, there are forage plants that don't mind having damp feet. Here is a shortlist.

Cuckooflower *Lady's Smock (Cardamine pratensis)*
This pretty little pale pink flower, much appreciated by honeybees, is a spring-flowering member of the Mustard family.

Gallberry *Inkberry (Ilex coriacea or glabra)*
A member of the Holly family, Gallberry is highly prized in the USA for honey production. It flowers in summer.

Giant Purple Hyssop *(Agastache scrophulariifolia)*
Impressively tall purple spires in summer and into the autumn offer both nectar and pollen to honeybees and other pollinators.

Marsh Marigold *Kingcup (Caltha palustris)*
An excellent source of early season forage for honeybees, these giant Buttercups are perfect for marshy ground.

Ragged Robin *(Lychnis flos-cuculi)*
Another denizen of marshes and wet ground, this pretty pink wild flower is a great source of summer forage.

Rosebay Willowherb *(Chamaenerion angustifolium)*
These tall spikes of pink flowers will grow virtually anywhere, including damp ground. They produce abundant pollen and nectar through the summer.

Swamp Milkweed *(Asclepias incarnata)*
Native to the USA, Swamp Milkweed flowers in summer and is
one of a large family of nectar-rich plants loved by honeybees.

Water Mint *(Mentha aquatica)*
Fragrant and beautiful, summer-flowering Water Mint is
popular with honeybees but has invasive tendencies, so should
be grown in a container sunk into the water's edge.

Watercress (*Nasturtium officinale*)
One of our favourite salad ingredients, watercress inhabits
streams and ponds. Flowering from summer in to early autumn,
it is a source of both pollen and nectar.

A pond can be a valuable source of water for honeybees, but they need
hard standing. Create this by placing flat stones at the water's edge or
by incorporating aquatic plants such as Frogbit to provide natural
'stepping stones'.

ROOF TERRACES

Gardening on rooftops poses special challenges for plants, as they are exposed to temperature fluctuations, wind and drought. It's important to favour hardy, wind-resistant varieties that are able to withstand such a harsh environment.

However, the advantage of gardening in containers, as most people do on roof terraces, is that you can easily replace failing plants or give them another chance in a more sheltered area. Screening (with wicker or bamboo panels, for example) offers shelter and provides structure for flowering climbers. The more you can avoid the chilling and drying effect of wind by screening, the wider variety of plants you'll be able to grow. You can also bring in pretty, bee-friendly annuals through spring and summer to augment more structured perennial plantings.

Roof terraces are incredibly productive spaces for growing fruit and vegetables, too, and can be the ideal place for 'tower' growing systems. These offer a large planting area on a small footprint. (See 'The Edible Garden' on page 87 and 'Resources' on page 117.)

SPRING

Allium, Alpine Aster, Astilbe, Borage, Bugle, Cranesbill/Hardy Geranium, Crocus, Delosperma, Grape Hyacinth, Heather, Hellebore, Pasque Flower, Poppy, Potentilla, Sea Pink, Star of Bethlehem, Sweet Pea, Wallflower

SUMMER

Agastache, Allium, Alpine Aster, Astilbe, Autumn Sage, Borage, Bugle, Carline Thistle, Common Fleabane, Common Knapweed, Coreopsis, Cranesbill/Hardy Geraniums, Dahlia (simple, open-centred varieties), Daylily, Delosperma, Fiddleneck, Flax, Heather, Lavender, Lilac Sage, Mullein, Oregano, Poppy, Pot Marigold, Hosta, Potentilla, Purple Coneflower, Russian Sage, Scabious, Sea Holly, Sea Pink, Stonecrop, Sweet Pea, Teasel, Viper's Bugloss, Wallflower, Yarrow

AUTUMN

Agastache, Autumn Crocus, Autumn Sage, Autumn Stonecrop, Borage, Carline Thistle, Common Fleabane, Cranesbill/Hardy Geraniums, Dahlia (simple, open-centred varieties), Delosperma, Fiddleneck, Heather, Oregano, Poppy, Pot Marigold, Purple Coneflower, Russian Sage, Scabious, Yarrow

WINTER INTO SPRING

Cyclamen, Heather, Hellebore, Rock Cress, Snowdrop, Sweet Violet, Wallflower, Winter Aconite, Winter Crocus, Winter Pansy

 CLIMBERS: Clematis, Climbing Hydrangea, climbing Nasturtium, Common Ivy, Japanese Wisteria, Passion Flower

 BUSHES AND SMALL TREES: Bearberry, Bluebeard, Ceanothus, Deutzia, Dogwood, Escallonia, Hebe, Lilac, Mahonia, Olive, Pyracantha, Rock Rose, Skimmia, Spirea, Viburnum, Shrubby Germander, Winter Honeysuckle

r: Wisteria

GREEN ROOFS

Good for buildings and good for people, green roof systems involve covering areas of a building's roof with plants. Benefits include mitigating the urban 'heat island' effect and improving run-off water quality, with the plants acting as a filter. And, if planted with the right species, they can be bee-friendly too.

Green roofs, though, are often 'green deserts', planted with a very limited range of species – commonly sedum, which flowers just once a year. This can be for financial reasons but often it's because people don't know how much more they could achieve. Knowledgeably planted to support pollinators and biodiversity, using a wide range of hardy species that thrive even in shallow substrates, a green roof can become productive, beautiful and sustainable, with multi-season forage for pollinators.

New York City's Department of Parks and Recreations has an extraordinary 'working laboratory' with more than 25 different green roof growing systems. (You can access this research in detail at nycgovparks.org.) By their reckoning, roofs in the five New York boroughs offer around 88 million sq m (944 million sq ft) of space, much of which is still available to be converted to green space. The roofscapes of London and other cities offer similar mind-blowing opportunities for urban greening.

Installing green roofs on new or existing buildings raises complex issues of physical systems, weight, water and plant choice. The selection of the correct substrate is also critical. This is not usually the province of amateur gardeners, but the good news is that an increasing number of expert green roof providers now offering pollinator-friendly plantings. (See Resources on pages 117–123.)

LIVING WALLS

Unlike green roofs systems, creating 'living walls' is totally feasible for any gardener. These vertical gardens are a brilliant way to achieve lush plantings with little or no footprint. This makes them perfect for so many situations, from balconies to large gardens.

The living walls we see in public spaces are often planted with what can only be described as 'green mackintosh' plants that offer no pollen or nectar. Being non-productive, they're cheaper to maintain and, to be fair, they do play an important role in greening the environment, thermal control (insulating and cooling buildings) and reducing carbon levels. (During the day plants absorb many harmful gases from the air, including the 'greenhouse gas', carbon dioxide.) But it would be good to see pollinator plantings pushed up the living wall agenda, especially in urban environments.

There are many different living wall approaches to consider for your garden, from sophisticated hydroponics to simple DIY systems using recycled containers. You'll find masses of specialist advice online.

The planting potential is huge. You can create anything from an abundant kitchen garden to a scented flower garden to elevate the senses. Here are a few honeybee-pleasing suggestions to get started with.

SPRING

Aubrieta, Candytuft, Chive, Crocus, Delosperma,
Forget-me-not, Heather, Hellebore, Rosemary, Pasque
Flower, Poppy, Sea Pink, Solomon's Seal, Strawberry,
Sweet Pea

SUMMER

Alyssum, Aster/Michaelmas Daisy, Autumn Sage,
Baby Blue Eyes, Basil, Bee Balm, Candytuft, Catmint,
Catnip, Chive, Delosperma, Dill, Dwarf Dahlia,
Forget-me-not, Heather, Heuchera, Jacob's Ladder,
Lavender, Mint, Nasturtium, Oregano, Phlox,
Poppy, Pot Marigold, Rosemary,
Salvia, Scabious, Sea Pink,
Serbian Bellflower, Strawberry,
Sweet Marjoram, Sweet
Mignonette, Sweet Pea,
Thyme, Tobacco Plant,
Verbena, Yarrow, Zinnia

AUTUMN

Aster/Michaelmas Daisy, Autumn Sage, Autumn
Stonecrop, Baby Blue Eyes, Bluebeard, Catmint,
Catnip, Delosperma, Dwarf Dahlia, Heather,
Nasturtium, Oregano, Phlox, Poppy, Pot Marigold,
Rosemary, Scabious, Sweet Marjoram, Sweet
Mignonette, Tobacco Plant, Verbena, Yarrow, Zinnia

WINTER
INTO SPRING

Cyclamen, Heather, Hellebore,
Rock Cress, Siberian Squill,
Snowdrop, Sweet Violet, Winter
Aconite, Winter Crocus,
Winter Pansy

l: Dill
r: Zinnia

THE EDIBLE GARDEN

One of the most exciting things about planting for honeybees is that it can go hand in hand with growing your own food. Nothing beats the thrill of growing, harvesting and eating freshly-picked produce.

Honeybees are thought to play a role in the production of one in every three mouthfuls of food we consume. Whether this is strictly true or not, it's indisputable that they are crucial to abundant cropping of many of the edible plants on which we rely. This is also true for the plants on which so many other insect species, birds and mammals depend for both food and habitats.

It's worth saying again here that you don't need a large plot to produce herbs, vegetables and some fruits. If you do have a big garden, of course, this can extend into a far greater range of fruits, and even include fruit and nut trees.

You can grow your own in anything from recycled tin cans to pots and tubs. Even more excitingly, you can also produce significant crops from living walls and from freestanding 'tower' growing systems, both of which occupy minimal floor areas, making them great for small spaces. (See Resources on pages 117–123 for more information.)

Here follows a shortlist of bee-friendly edibles. Some of these plants are self-pollinating, but they will yield far more if visited by honeybees.

Many edibles such as artichokes, carrots, beetroots,
onions and brassicas (e.g. cabbages and cauliflower) are
harvested for eating before they flower. So, for the sake
of the bees, the answer is to share the crop. Plant a bit
more than you need, so that you can take some for your
kitchen and leave some unpicked, to flower for the bees.

HERBS: Angelica, Basil, Bergamot, Borage, Camomile, Caraway, Chervil, Chicory, Chive, Comfrey, Common Mallow, Common Yarrow, Coriander, Dill, Fennel, Hyssop, Lavender, Lemon Balm, Lovage, Mint, Nasturtium, Oregano, Parsley, Purslane, Rocket, Rosemary, Sage, Summer Savory, Sweet Cicely, Thyme, Winter Savory

VEGETABLES: Asparagus, Aubergine, Beans (e.g. Broad Bean, French Bean, Runner Bean), Beetroot, Bell Pepper, Broccoli, Brussels Sprouts, Cabbage, Cardoon, Carrot, Cauliflower, Celery, Chilli Pepper, Chinese Cabbage, Courgette, Cucumber, Garlic, Globe Artichoke, Jerusalem Artichoke, Kohlrabi, Marrow, Melon, Okra, Onion, Parsnip, Peas, Pumpkin (and many other squashes), Turnip

FRUITING BUSHES AND VINES: Bilberry, Blackberry, Blackcurrant, Blackthorn (Sloe), Dog Rose (Rose Hips), Grapes, Kiwi Fruit, Loganberry, Passion Fruit, Raspberry, Redcurrant, Strawberry, Whitecurrant

FRUIT AND NUT TREES: Almond, Apple, Apricot, Cherry, Crab Apple, Hazelnut, Lemon, Medlar, Orange, Peach, Pear, Plum, Quince, Rowan, Walnut, White Mulberry

r: Apple Tree

THE WILDFLOWER QUESTION

In recent years, the role of wildflowers in feeding honeybees has been widely misunderstood. Yes, wildflowers are a precious resource. Yes, there are not nearly enough of them. But no, they are not going to save the day. No matter how many packets of bee-friendly wildflower seeds are nobly given out and scattered, they are just not going to supply enough forage to turn the tide. They simply cannot make up for all the lost broadleaf woodland, grubbed-up hedgerows, close-mown lawns, tidied-up railway embankments and hard-landscaped gardens that rob the environment of what many might call 'weeds'.

Honeybees evolved as tree-dwellers, so it's not surprising that their main source of forage is still flowering trees and bushes. However, in recent times media messaging has overlooked this fact, setting an agenda all about wildflowers, seed bombs and 'wildflower meadows'.

Ah … the wildflower meadow, a totem of our times. Here's the thing about wildflower meadows. Although composed of wildflowers, they are far from 'wild'. In fact, they are managed environments that need to be either eaten off by grazing animals or mown at specific intervals to avoid them becoming overgrown with dominant species (such as tall grasses and Nettles) and to allow smaller species (such as Bird's Foot Trefoil and Selfheal) to flourish, keeping everything in balance.

A wildflower meadow composed of the wrong plant species, planted in the wrong soil or not properly managed will quickly be lost to invasive or competitive species, becoming just another testament to good intentions but poor understanding. There are many exemplary wildflower meadows you can visit for inspiration; behind them is the expert knowledge of enlightened farmers, gardeners and horticulturalists.

So, speaking personally, as beekeepers who are simply trying to create maximum forage for honeybees, here's where we stand on wildflowers. We literally can't get enough of them. Nor can the bees. We'd love everyone to mow less often, to allow wild species to flourish in shaggy grass. We love wildflower patches, meadows and margins rich with simple, native species.

But we'd also welcome the broader understanding that – in the bigger picture – wildflowers alone cannot supply the sheer bulk and variety of multi-season forage needed to sustain bee colonies. This will always be largely provided by trees and bushes, augmented by smaller plants of many different types.

Phew – lecture over! Now for a list of some important wild flowers for honeybees.

Bird's Foot Trefoil
A member of the pea family, Bird's Foot Trefoil is a classic component of wildflower seed mixes, providing both pollen and nectar during the summer months.

Bramble
Flowering from late spring to early summer, Wild Blackberry bushes provide a feast for honeybees. Well-pollinated, they later produce abundant blackberry crops to feed birds and other wildlife. And – if you're quick – people, too.

Daisies
From tiny lawn Daisies to the abundant Ox-Eyes flowering profusely by the roadside in early summer, daisies are a luscious resource for bees.

Dandelion
The chrome yellow burst of Dandelions is a joyous signal of spring. One of the most valuable plants for honeybees, dandelions give precious early-season pollen and nectar.

Dog Rose
This wild climbing rose offers simple, abundant flowers in summer followed by rose hips that feed birds, squirrels and many other creatures, and are a rich source of Vitamin C.

Rosebay Willowherb
A staple of waste ground and derelict buildings, this 'fireweed' (it's well known for colonising areas scorched by fire) is one of honeybees' richest food sources in summer.

Viper's Bugloss
Where many flowers have their nectar flow in the middle of the day, the nectar from Viper's Bugloss' dense blue spires offers a dependable feast throughout the day. Summer-flowering.

White Clover
Once upon a time, Clover was grown as a cash crop and was a mainstay of English honey production. Nowadays, it is rarely grown commercially, but it thrives as a valuable wildflower, blooming throughout the summer.

Wild Geranium *Cranesbill*

Honeybees will choose Cranesbill's unassuming flowers time and again, preferring them to many more showy plants in bloom. Depending on the species, these wild forms will flower from late spring until early autumn.

'WILD' LAWNS

One of the simplest and most beautiful ways to add to bee forage in the larger garden is to change the way you think about lawns. Once upon a time, they had to be emerald green and close-mown with military precision. Nowadays, I think we can all live with the idea that not all grassy areas have to look like cricket pitches.

Here are some simple approaches:

• Stop using pesticides and lawn fertilisers (perennial wildflowers, which go on from year to year, dislike rich soil).

• Mow less often to allow Daisies, Dandelions, Clovers, Selfheal, Plantains and other small wildflowers to establish. These are super-important to honeybees.

• Add in wildflower plants or seed wildflower patches into the lawn. Use a combination of perennials and annuals if you want the patch to last.

- Plant bee-friendly spring bulbs such as Crocus, Grape Hyacinth and Snowdrop into the lawn. If you plant them in strips or clumps you can close-mow the rest of the grass.

- Allow lawn margins to get shaggy and just see what starts to grow. Or speed things up by sowing with a hardy, native wildflower mix. Mow the margins just twice a year, in spring and again at the end of autumn.

- Plant a Clover lawn instead of grass. You can walk on it (although it won't stand up to a lot of wear and tear), it will look and smell beautiful all through the summer and only need mowing a couple of times a year. For low-traffic areas, lawns planted with ground-hugging Thymes are another bee-friendly alternative to grass, with fragrant flowers in mid-summer.

- If you want to go the whole hog and turn a large area of mown grass over to a sustainable wildflower meadow, either work with a professional or research the subject very thoroughly to find exactly the right mix of species for your soil and locality. You will also need to learn how to manage the meadow so that it will thrive and evolve with all the grasses and wildflowers in balance for many years to come. Pollinators of all sorts will reward your effort.

PLANT WITH CAUTION!

Plants to be wary of come in two types. There are those that have been noted as (sometimes or always) toxic to honeybees – (e.g. Lobster Claws and Trumpet Flower). Then there are those that make odd-tasting honey (e.g. Privet and Strawberry Tree, both known for their bitter taste) or honey that's toxic to humans – e.g. honey made largely or exclusively from Bog Rosemary, Mountain Laurel, Rhododendrons and Azaleas.

PLANTS TOXIC TO HONEYBEES AND/OR THAT PRODUCE TOXIC/ UNPLEASANT-TASTING HONEY

FLOWERS
- Belladonna/Jersey Lily
- Buttercup
- Deadly Nightshade
- Henbane
- Lobster Claws
- Stargazer Lily
- Trumpet Flower *Angel's Trumpet*

SHRUBS
- Azalea
- Bog Rosemary
- Common Box
- Mountain Laurel
- Oleander
- Privet
- Rhododendron
- Yellow Jessamine

TREES
- Balsa
- California Horse Chestnut *California Buckeye*
- Chinese Lime
- Flame of the Forest *African Tulip Tree*
- New Zealand Laurel *Karaka Tree*
- Silver Lime
- Strawberry Tree
- Weeping Silver Lime

CHAPTER SEVEN

TEN
OF THE
BEST

S o you just want to get started as quickly as possible! Here are 'Ten of the Best' recommendations for flowers, shrubs, climbers and trees that are nectar-and-pollen magnets for honeybees.

I've brought them together from a wide range of expert sources, including beekeepers' personal observations, as well as academic field studies, and invaluable listings from the Royal Horticultural Society and bee charities such as The BBKA (British Beekeepers Association).

The following lists are not exhaustive, but they will be a real help in compiling rapid shopping lists. Remember, though, to check site suitability and eventual plant sizes, especially with shrubs and trees.

Where you see this symbol ❂ it tells you that specifically bee-friendly cultivars of that plant are available. Buy from nurseries that indicate which of their plants are bee-friendly or check on the RHS website (see Resources page 118).

The flowering seasons given are for the Northern Hemisphere. If you're in a different part of the world, please check online.

TEN OF THE BEST FLOWERS

NAME	EXPERTS RECOMMEND	FLOWERING SEASON
ALLIUM	*Allium giganteum* Giant Onion *Allium schoenoprasum* Chives *Nectaroscordum siculum* Sicilian Honey Garlic	May–June May–August June

BORAGE/
BUGLOSS
	Borago officinalis Borage Herb/
	   Starflower
	Echium vulgare Viper's bugloss ✿
	Anchusa azurea Garden
	   Anchusa/Italian Bugloss ✿
	Echium plantagineum Purple Viper's
	   bugloss ✿
		April–October
		
		June–August
		June–September
		
		June–September

CONEFLOWER	*Echinacea purpurea* Purple Coneflower *Rudbeckia hirta* Black-Eyed Susan ✿	July–September July–October

CRANESBILL
*Cranesbill
(Hardy
Geranium)*
	Geranium sanguineum
	   Bloody Cranesbill ✿
	Geranium maculatum Spotted
	   Cranesbill ✿
	Geranium pratense Meadow
	   Cranesbill ✿
		May–June
		
		May–August
		
		June–September

DAISY	*Leucanthemum vulgare* Ox-Eye Daisy *Erigeron speciousus* Aspen Fleabane ✿ *Aster amellus* European Michaelmas Daisy ✿	June–August June–August August–October

NAME	EXPERTS RECOMMEND	FLOWERING SEASON
HEATHER	*Erica carnea* Alpine Heath ♥	January–April
	Erica cinerea Bell Heather ♥	June–September
	Calluna vulgaris Ling ♥	August–September
HELENIUM *Sneezeweed*	*Helenium bigelovii* Bigelow's Sneezeweed	June–September
	Helenium 'Sahin's Early Flowerer'	June–September
	Helenium autumnale ♥	August–September
LAVENDER	*Lavandula angustifolia* English Lavender ♥	June–August
	Lavandula x *intermedia* 'Hidcote Giant'	July–August
	Lavandula x *chaytoriae* 'Sawyers'	July–August
SAGE/ SALVIA	*Salvia officinalis* Sage Herb	June–August
	Salvia x sylvestris Violet Sage, Wood Sage ♥	June–August
	Perovskia atriplicifolia Russian Sage	July–October
THISTLE	*Cirsium vulgare* Spear Thistle	June–July
	Cynara cardunculus Cardoon/Globe Artichoke	June–September
	Echinops ritro Globe Flower/Blue Hedgehog ♥	July–August

TEN OF THE BEST CLIMBERS

NAME	EXPERTS RECOMMEND	FLOWERING SEASON
BOSTON IVY	*Parthenocissus tricuspidata*	June–August
CLEMATIS	*Clematis armandii* *Clematis vitalba* Old Man's Beard, Traveller's Joy *Clematis cirrhosa* Evergreen Clematis ☉	March–May July–September December–February
CLIMBING HYDRANGEA	*Hydrangea anomala* subsp. *petiolaris*	June–July
IVY	*Hedera colchica* 'Dentata Variegata' Persian Ivy *Hedera helix* Common Ivy ☉	September–November September–November
PASSION FLOWER	*Passiflora incarnata* *Passiflora caerulea* *Passiflora edulis*	June–September June–October June–October
CLIMBING ROSE	*Rosa* 'Polyantha Grandiflora' *Rosa filipes* 'Kiftsgate' *Rosa moschata* Musk Rose	June–July July–August July–August
THUNBERGIA *Black-Eyed Susan Vine*	*Thunbergia alata* 'Superstar Orange' *Thunbergia alata* 'Susie Series'	June–October June–October
VINE LILAC	*Hardenbergia violacea*	February–April
VIRGINIA CREEPER	*Parthenocissus quinquefolia* *Parthenocissus henryana* Chinese Virginia Creeper	June–July June–August
WISTERIA	*Wisteria floribunda* Japanese Wisteria *Wisteria sinensis* Chinese Wisteria	May–June May–June

TEN OF THE BEST SHRUBS

NAME	EXPERTS RECOMMEND	FLOWERING SEASON
ABELIA	*Abelia parvifolia* Schumann Abelia *Abelia* 'Edward Goucher'	May–September
BRAMBLE	*Rubus fruticosus* Wild Blackberry	May–June
BUDDLEJA *Butterfly Bush*	*Buddleja davidii* ♥ *Buddleja globosa* Orange Ball Tree	July–September June
CEANOTHUS *Californian Lilac*	*Ceonothus* 'Autumnal Blue' *Ceonothus thrysiflorus* var. *repens* Creeping Blue Blossom	August–October May–June
HEBE	*Hebe brachysiphon* *Hebe* 'Autumn Glory'	May–June July–October
PHILADELPHUS *Mock Orange*	*Philadelphus* 'Beauclerk' *Philadelphus microphyllus*	June–July June–July
ROSEMARY	*Rosmarinus officinalis* ♥ *Rosmarinus officinalis* 'Miss Jessopp's Upright'	April–June *NB May repeat flower at other times, e.g. December–February* May–June
SNOWBERRY	*Symphoricarpos albus* Common Snowberry *Symphoricarpos occidentalis* Wolfberry *Symphoricarpos orbiculatus* Coralberry	June–August June–August August–September
VIBURNUM	*Viburnum lantana* Wayfaring Tree *Viburnum plicatum f. tomentosum* ♥	May–June May–June
WILD ROSE	*Rosa canina* Dog Rose *Rosa rugosa* Japanese Rose ♥	May–June June–September

TEN OF THE BEST TREES

NAME	EXPERTS RECOMMEND	FLOWERING SEASON
BEE-BEE TREE	*Tetradium daniellii*	August–September
CHERRY	*Prunus padus* Bird Cherry *Prunus* x *yedoensis* Yoshino Cherry *Prunus* x *subhirtella* 'Autumnalis' Winter-flowering Cherry	April–May April–May November–March
FALSE ACACIA Robinia	*Robinia hispida* Rose Acacia	May–June

HAWTHORN	*Crataegus laevigata* Midland
	  Hawthorn ❤
	Crataegus monogyna
	Crataegus persimilis 'Prunifolia'
	  Broad-leaved Cockspur Thorn
		May
		
		May
		May

HORSE CHESTNUT	*Aesculus hippocastanum* *Aesculus* x *carnea* Red Horse Chestnut *Aesculus indica* Indian Horse Chestnut	April–May May May
INDIAN BEAN TREE	*Catalpa bignonioides*	July–August
JAPANESE PAGODA TREE	*Styphnolobium japonicum*	August–September *NB This tree will take many years to flower*
LIME Linden	*Tilia cordata* Small-leaved Lime *Tilia* x *europaea* Common Lime *Tilia platyphyllos* Broad-leaved Lime	July July July
MAPLE	*Acer campestre* Field Maple	April–May
WILLOW	*Salix daphnoides* Violet Willow *Salix caprea* Goat Willow ❤	February–March March–April

CHAPTER EIGHT

REMARKABLE FACTS ABOUT HONEYBEES

The more we learn about honeybees, the more fascinating they are. They live not as individuals, but as a super-organism in a perfectly ordered society and they are in every way adapted to live purposeful and productive lives without wasting time, energy or natural resources. Here are a few glimpses into their complex world.

1 Of an estimated 25,000 known species of bee worldwide, only seven species are honeybees.

2 Honeybees have been on earth, making honey, for about 100 million years. (Modern humans have only been around for a fraction of that time – around 200,000 years.)

3 Honeybees are unique in storing honey to allow them to overwinter as a colony or to survive lean times. No other type of bee does this.

4 Honeybees pollinate a significant percentage of our vegetables, fruit and flowers. Efficient pollination leads to better cropping, feeding not just people, but also many animals, birds and insects.

5 Honeybees evolved as tree-dwellers and still need to gather the majority of their forage from trees and shrubs rather than from garden flowers or wildflowers.

6 Honeybees are vegetarians. They visit flowers to gather pollen (protein to feed their brood) and nectar (carbohydrate for energy), which they turn into honey to feed adult bees as well as to lay down as winter stores. Every year, each hive needs to gather around 50kg (110lb) of pollen and 200kg (440lb) of nectar just to survive before any honey crop can be taken.

7 All worker bees are female. Male bees (drones) do no work in the hive; their sole purpose in life is to fertilise a queen.

8 Honeybees' antennae detect sound and vibration and give them an amazing sense of smell, allowing them to detect specific forage sources up to 1.5km (1 mile) away. They also use them like cats' whiskers, as a physical gauge of space.

9 Honeybees tend to forage within a 4.5-km (3-mile) radius of their hive. They can fly farther afield, but the energy requirement to do this leads to diminishing returns for the hive. They navigate using a variety of means, including physical landmarks, the position of the sun (which their polarising eyes allow them to see even on cloudy days) and a magnetoreceptor in their abdomen that senses the Earth's magnetic field.

10 Scout bees locate sources of forage and return to the hive with samples to share. If the samples pass muster, the scouts then communicate the source's whereabouts by 'waggle dancing' the directions to their sisters.

11 Honeybees have five eyes: a large compound eye on either side of their head and three small eyes (ocelli) on the top of their head that act as a navigation system. They see in colour, but are most sensitive to the blue end of the spectrum and into ultraviolet. Hairs between the compound lenses detect wind conditions, helping them stay on course.

12 An individual honeybee visits 100 or more flowers in a single foraging trip. Unlike many other pollinators, honeybees will only forage on a single type of flower on any one trip.

Flowers give off a positive electrical charge for some time after being visited by a bee, and the bees also leave a chemical 'footprint'. These and additional signals alert other pollinators not to bother visiting that bloom for nectar at that time.

 Honeybees will visit about two million flowers and fly around 80,000km (50,000 miles) to make a 454-g (1-lb) jar of honey.

 During its entire lifetime, a single foraging bee will collect enough nectar to make one-twelfth of a teaspoon of honey.

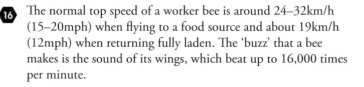 The normal top speed of a worker bee is around 24–32km/h (15–20mph) when flying to a food source and about 19km/h (12mph) when returning fully laden. The 'buzz' that a bee makes is the sound of its wings, which beat up to 16,000 times per minute.

Year round, the bees keep the core hive temperature at between 32°C and 35°C (90 and 95°F). In hot weather, they dispel heat by fanning their wings. In winter, they isolate their flight muscles, using them to generate heat through 'shivering' without wing motion.

In high summer, a busy hive can contain as many as 70,000 female worker bees, plus the queen and several thousand drones (males). In winter, the colony will drop to around a quarter of its summer size.

Spring- and summer-born worker bees perform a series of predetermined jobs during their five- to six-week lifespan (bees born in the autumn will live through the winter until spring). In the first three weeks of their lives, they progress from cleaning the comb and feeding larvae to receiving pollen and nectar from incoming bees. Other jobs include beeswax production. Only in the last stage of their lives do they leave the hive to work as a forager.

 20 Bees do not hibernate. In autumn, the female workers throw the drones out of the hive to avoid feeding them through winter. The remaining colony clusters around the queen and will fly whenever the outside temperature is above 10°C (50°F).

21 Drones die in the process of mating, which takes place in flight. The queen makes just one nuptial trip in her life, during the course of which she will mate with many drones. She collects a lifetime supply of sperm, which she stores in her abdomen.

22 The queen is larger than the workers and has a fertile life of three to four years. Her key function is to lay eggs, which she does mainly in the spring and early summer, peaking at the summer solstice in June, when she might be laying as many as 2,000 eggs a day. As she is unable to care for herself, attendant bees follow her around to feed her, groom her and take away her waste.

23 Every queen has her own unique pheromone 'signature' which is spread throughout the hive from bee to bee. Amongst their many functions, her pheromones act as a 'password' so that intruder bees from other hives can quickly be recognised.

Anatomy of a honeybee

♀

a. antenna ; b. compound eye ; c. ocelli ; d. thorax ; e. wing ; f. abdomen ;
g. hind leg ; h. pollen press ; i. middle leg ; j. fore leg ; k. proboscis (tongue)

CHAPTER NINE

RESOURCES

There is a tremendous amount of information out there, especially online. Some of it simple and accessible… much of it deeply confusing and contradictory.

The links I've given you here are good starting places to explore the world of honeybees and find help and inspiration on a wide range of bee-related topics.

NOWHERE TO PLANT?

Planting forage is the single most important way that you can help honeybees. If you don't have anywhere to grow plants, consider volunteering or setting up a community gardening project. Public spaces such as golf courses, housing estates, public parks and sports pitches are often 'green deserts' with acres of mown lawns, some token flower beds and little or nothing to offer pollinators. Usually, though, they have margins or forgotten corners where bee-friendly plantings could be established. Often, too, no one has ever approached the groundkeepers or gardeners to ask whether they would be amenable to working with a community gardening group to improve biodiversity in their area. Look around your neighbourhood and see where you can make a difference.

Bermondsey Street Bees have undertaken a wide variety of community projects around our London hives, greening spaces from neglected graveyards to lacklustre council estates. We tend to focus on planting edible species, bringing a direct benefit to people as well as honeybees, birds, mammals and other insects.

The Royal Horticultural Society (RHS) website can connect you with local gardening groups or advise you on setting up your own. Many local councils and some charities also offer funding for greening projects. See **rhs.org.uk/communities** You can find and apply for a local allotment at **gov.uk/apply-allotment**

Other useful community gardening links include: **farmgarden.co.uk** and **groundworks.org.uk**

WANT TO BE A BEEKEEPER?

Hopefully, after reading this book, you will know that, in some parts of the country, more honeybees are *not* what the environment needs. Providing forage for existing bees should always be a priority. This becomes especially important if you are considering acquiring your own hives – and crucial if they are in an urban environment.

If you are truly drawn to beekeeping and prepared to take on the time commitment and responsibility it entails, then welcome to the craft! Your first step is to join your local beekeeping association to receive proper training and mentoring. Beekeeping is a lifelong learning experience and you need the knowledge and skills imparted by wise teachers.

If you can't have hives of your own, you can always volunteer to help local beekeepers once you have completed your basic training. (They will always prefer to have trained help.)

To find your local beekeeping association and other advice contact The British Beekeepers Association. The BBKA also runs an 'Adopt a Hive' scheme.
bbka.org.uk/join_us/

(Wales **wbka.com** | Scotland: **scottishbeekeepers.org.uk** | Ulster: **ubka.org**)

OTHER USEFUL RESOURCES

BEE CHARITIES/INFORMATION
The British Beekeepers Association: **bbka.org.uk**
Bees for Development: **beesfordevelopment.org**
International Bee Research Association: **ibrabee.org.uk**
The Honeybee Conservancy: **thehoneybeeconservacy.org**
Planet Bee Foundation: **planetbee.org**

ONLINE BEE-FRIENDLY PLANT
BUYING /INFORMATION
beehappyplants.co.uk
britishwildflowermeadowseeds.co.uk
dobies.co.uk (organic range)
jekkasherbfarm.com
meadowmania.co.uk
quickrop.co.uk
rhs.org.uk/perfectforpollinators
rosybee.com
seedsofitaly.com (organic range)
verticalveg.org.uk (blog)
wildflower.co.uk
wildflowerturf.co.uk

SYSTEM SUPPLIERS/CONSULTANTS

LIVING WALLS
treebox.co.uk
gardenbeet.com (based in Australia, will ship to UK)
biotecture.uk.com

GREEN ROOFS
greenroofshelters.co.uk
livingroofs.org
sky-garden.co.uk

GREEN INFRASTRUCTURE PROJECTS
ecologyconsultancy.co.uk

TOWER GROWING SYSTEMS
gardentowerproject.co.uk

SOME BEE-FRIENDLY GARDENS TO VISIT/ LEARNING EXPERIENCES

Look online to find bee-friendly gardens at home or abroad. There are inspirational Botanical Gardens all over the world and other 'must sees' include Piet Oudolph's wonderful plantings on New York's Highline.

Carr House Meadows, *Yorkshire*
Eden Project, *Cornwall*
Greenwich Peninsular Ecology Park, *London*
Highgrove Royal Gardens, *Gloucestershire*
Kew Gardens, *London*
National Beekeeping Centre, Stoneleigh Park, *Warwickshire*
National Beekeeping Centre Wales, *Conwy*
National Botanic Garden of Wales, *Carmarthenshire*
Oudolph Field, Hauser & Wirth Gallery, *Somerset*
Potters Fields Park, *London*
RHS Garden Harlow Carr, *Yorkshire*
RHS Garden Rosemoor, *Devon*
RHS Garden Wisley, *Surrey*
Sissinghurst Castle Garden, *Kent*
St Andrews Botanic Gardens, *Scotland*

GOOD READING

This is a short and very personal selection from my own library. It includes issues around honeybees, biodiversity, food campaigning and, of course, some good solid reference books on choosing plants. Some are out of print but available from second-hand booksellers, especially online.

Brickell, Christopher, Editor in Chief, *The RHS Encyclopedia of Plants & Flowers* (Dorling Kindersley, 2010, 5th Ed, ISBN 978-1-4053-5423-3)

Crane, Eva, *The World History of Beekeeping and Honey Hunting* (Gerald Duckworth & Co Ltd, 1999, ISBN 978-071562-827-0)

Ellis, Hattie, *Sweetness & Light: The Mysterious History of the Honey Bee* (Sceptre, 2005, new edition, ISBN 978-034073-452-0)

Goulson, Dave, *A Sting in the Tale: My Adventures with Bumblebees* (Jonathan Cape, 2013, ISBN 978-0-22409-689-8)

Gowing, Elizabeth, *Travels in Blood and Honey* (Signal Books, 2011, ISBN 978-1-904955-90-0)

Hooper, Ted and Taylor, Mike, *The Bee Friendly Garden* (Alphabet and Image, 2006, ISBN 1-899296-29-8)

Kirk, W.D.J., and Howes, F.N., *Plants for Bees: A Guide to the Plants that Benefit the Bees of the British Isles* (International Bee Research Association, 2012, ISBN 978-0-86098-271-5)

Packer, Sarit & Srulovich, Itamar, *Honey & Co, Food from the Middle East* (Saltyard Books, 2014, ISBN 978-1-444-75476-4)

Petrini, Carlo, *Food & Freedom: How the Slow Food Movement is Changing the World Through Gastronomy* (Rizzoli Ex Libris, 2015, ISBN 978-0-8478-4685-6)

Willes, Margaret, *The Gardens of The British Working Class* (Yale University Press, 2015, ISBN 978-0-300-21235-8)

The National Pollinator Strategy
Department for the Environment, Food & Rural Affairs
Online with downloadable factsheets at **www.gov.uk**

INDEX OF COMMON AND LATIN NAMES

Common names for plants can vary widely, depending on region and country. In many cases the most widely used name for a plant is also its Latin name.

KEY

♥ *Species have bee-friendly cultivars*

⚠ *Plants toxic to honeybees and/or produce toxic/unpleasant-tasting honey*

spp. *Various species*

A

Abelia, *Abelia* spp. ♥
African Tulip Tree, *see* Flame of the Forest
Agastache, *Agastache* spp. ♥
Alder, *Alnus glutinosa*
Allium (Ornamental Onion), *Allium* spp. ♥
Almond, *Prunus dulcis* ♥
Alpine Aster, *Aster alpinus*
Alpine Heath, *Erica carnea*
Alyssum (Sweet Alison, Sweet Alyssum), *Lobularia maritima* ♥
Amaryllis, *Hippeastrum* spp. ⚠
Angel's Trumpet, *see* Trumpet Flower
Angelica, *Angelica archangelica*
Apple, *Malus domestica* ♥

Apricot, *Prunus armeniaca* ✿
Aquilegia (Columbine), *Aquilegia* spp. ✿
Arnica, *Arnica montana*
Asparagus, *Asparagus officinalis* ✿
Aspen Fleabane, *Erigeron speciousus*
Aster/Michaelmas Daisy, *Aster* spp.
  and *Symphyotrichum* spp. ✿
Astilbe (False Goat's Beard), *Astilbe* spp. ✿
Astrantia (Masterwort), *Astrantia major* ✿
Aubergine, *Solanum melongena* ✿
Aubrieta, *Aubrieta* spp. ✿
Autumn Clematis, *Clematis terniflora*
Autumn Crocus, *Colchicum autumnale, C. agrippinum*
Autumn Hawkbit, *Scorzoneroides autumnalis*
Autumn Ox-Eye Daisy, *Leucanthemella serotina*
Autumn Sage, *Salvia greggii* ✿
Autumn Stonecrop, *Sedum* spp. and *Hylotelephium* spp. ✿
Azalea, *Rhododendron* spp. ⚠

B

Baby Blue Eyes, *Nemophila menziesii*
Baby's Breath, *see* Gypsophila
Balsa Tree, *Ochroma pyramidale* ⚠
Barberry, *see* Berberis
Basil, *Ocimum basilicum*
Batchelor's Buttons, *see* Cornflower
Bearberry, *Arctostaphylos uva-ursi*
Beautyberry, *see* Callicarpa
Bee Balm, *Monarda* spp. ✿
Bee Bee Tree (Evodia), *Tetradium daniellii*
Beetroot, *Beta vulgaris* 'Crimson King'
Bell Heather, *Erica cinerea*
Bell Pepper (Sweet Pepper), *Capsicum annuum* var. *annuum*

Berberis (Barberry), *Berberis thunbergii* ☯

Bergamot (herb), *Monarda didyma*

Bilberry, *Vaccinium myrtillus*

Bird Cherry, *Prunus padus*

Bird's Foot Trefoil, *Lotus corniculatus*

Blackberry, *see* Wild Blackberry

Blackcurrant, *Ribes nigrum* ☯

Black-Eyed Susan, *Rudbeckia fulgida, R. hirta* ☯

Black-Eyed Susan Vine, *Thunbergia alata* ☯

Blackthorn (Sloe), *Prunus spinosa*

Blanket Flower, *Gaillardia* spp. ☯

Bleeding Heart, *Dicentra* spp. ☯

Bloody Cranesbill, *Geranium sanguineum*

Bluebeard, *Caryopteris* x *clandonensis* ☯

Blue Hedgehog, *see* Globe Flower

Bodnant Viburnum, *Viburnum × bodnantense* ☯

Bog Rosemary, *Andromeda polifolia* ⚠

Borage (Starflower), *Borago officinalis*

Box (Common Box), *Buxus sempervirens* (Not poisonous to bees,
   but honey made from it can be toxic to humans) ⚠

Bramble, *see* Wild Blackberry

Broad Bean, *Vicia faba*

Broad-leaved Cockspur Thorn, *Crataegus persimilis* 'Prunifolia'

Broad-leaved Lime, *Tilia platyphyllos*

Broccoli, *Brassica oleracea* (Italica Group)

Broom, *Cytisus scoparius* and other *Cytisus* spp.

Brussels Sprouts, *Brassica oleracea* (Gemmifera Group) ☯

Buddleja (Butterfly Bush), *Buddleja* spp. ☯

Bugbane, *Actaea simplex* ☯

Bugle, *Ajuga reptans*

Bull Thistle, *see* Spear Thistle

Buttercup, *Ranunculus acris* ⚠

Button Snakewort, *see* Liatris

C

Cabbage, *Brassica oleracea* (Capitata Group) ☻
California Buckeye, *see* California Horse Chestnut
California Horse Chestnut (California Buckeye),
   Aesculus californica ⚠
Californian Lilac, *see* Ceanothus
Candytuft, *Iberis* spp. ☻
Caraway, *Carum carvi*
Cardoon, *see* Globe Artichoke
Carline Thistle, *Carlina vulgaris*
Carrot, *Daucus carota* subsp. *sativus* ☻
Catmint, *Nepeta* x *faassenii, N. racemosa* ☻
Catnip, *Nepeta cataria*
Cauliflower, *Brassica oleracea* (Botrytis Group) ☻
Ceanothus (Californian Lilac), *Ceanothus* spp. ☻
Callicarpa (Beautyberry), *Callicarpa bodinieri* ☻
Celery, *Apium graveolens* ☻
Chamomile, *Chamaemelum nobile*
Cherry, *Prunus avium* (Wild Cherry) ☻,
   P. padus (Bird Cherry) ☻
Chervil, *Anthriscus cerefolium*
Chicory, *Cichorium intybus*
Chilli Pepper, *Capsicum annum* ☻
Chinese Cabbage, *Brassica rapa* (Pekinensis Group) ☻
Chinese Lime, *Tilia oliveri* ⚠
Chinese Virginia Creeper, *Parthenocissus henryana*
Chinese Wisteria, *Wisteria sinensis*
Chives, *Allium schoenoprasum*
Christmas Rose, *see* Hellebore
Cinquefoil, *see* Potentilla
Clematis, *Clematis* spp. ☻
Climbing Bean, *see* Green Bean

Clover, *Trifolium pratense* (Red Clover), *T. repens* (White Clover)

Coltsfoot, *Tussilago farfara*

Columbine, *see* Aquilegia

Comfrey, *Symphytum officinale*

Common Box, *see* Box

Common Fleabane, *Pulicaria dysenterica*

Common Holly, *Ilex aquifolium* spp. ☯ (Not all hollies flower, check before buying)

Common Knapweed, *Centaurea nigra*

Common Lime, *Tilia* x *europaea*

Common Marigold, *see* Pot Marigold

Common Mallow, *Malva sylvestris*

Common Sage, *see* Sage

Common Snowberry, *Symphoricarpos albus*

Common Tansy (Tansy), *Tanacetum vulgare*

Common Yarrow, *Achillea millefolium*

Coralberry, *Symphoricarpos orbiculatus*

Coreopsis (Tickseed), *Coreopsis* spp. ☯

Coriander, *Coriandrum sativum*

Cornflower (Batchelor's Buttons), *Centaurea cyanus*

Cosmos, *Cosmos* spp. ☯

Cotoneaster, *Cotoneaster* spp. ☯

Courgette, *Cucurbita pepo* var. *cylindrica* ☯

Cowslip, *Primula veris*

Crab apple, *Malus sylvestris* and other *Malus* cultivars

Cranesbill/Hardy Geranium, *Geranium* spp. ☯, *Geranium lucidum* (Shining Cranesbill), *G. mollis* (Dove's Foot Cranesbill), *G. robertianum* (Herb Robert)

Crocus, *Crocus* spp. ☯

Cuckoo Flower (Lady's Smock), *Cardamine pratensis*

Cucumber, *Cucumis sativus* ☯

Culver's Root, *Veronicastrum virginicum* ☯

Currant, Flowering, *Ribes sanguineum* ☯

Currant, Fruiting, (black, white and red), *Ribes* spp. ✿
Cyclamen (Sowbread), *Cyclamen* spp. ✿

D

Dahlia, *Dahlia* spp. ✿ (Any simple, open-flowered cultivars)
Dandelion, *Taraxacum officinale*
Daylily, *Hemerocallis* spp. ✿
Deadly Nightshade, *Atropa belladonna* ⚠
Deadnettle, *Lamium album* (White Deadnettle), *L. purpureum*
  (Red Deadnettle), *L. maculatum* (Spotted Deadnettle)
Daisy (Lawn Daisy), *Bellis perennis*
Delosperma, *Delosperma* spp. ✿
Deutzia, *Deutzia* spp. ✿
Dill, *Anethum graveolens*
Dog Rose, *Rosa canina*

E

Elderflower, *Sambucus nigra*
Elecampane, *Inula helenium*
English Bluebell, *Hyacinthoides non-scripta* (Avoid the highly
  invasive Spanish Bluebell, *H. hispanica*)
English Lavender, *Lavandula angustifolia*
Escallonia, *Escallonia* spp. ✿
Eucalyptus (Gum Tree), *Eucalyptus* spp.
Eucryphia, *Eucryphia* spp. ✿
Euphorbia, *Euphorbia* spp. ✿
European Michaelmas Daisy, *Aster amellus*
Evening Primrose, *Oenothera biennis*
Evergreen Clematis, *Clematis cirrhosa*

F

False Acacia, *Robinia pseudoacacia*

False Goat's Beard, *see* Astilbe
False Indigo, *Baptisia australis*
Farewell to Spring, *see* Godetia
Fatsia Japonica (Japanese Aralia), *Fatsia japonica* ☻
Fennel, *Foeniculum vulgare*
Feverfew, *Tanacetum parthenium*
Fiddleneck, *Phacelia tanacetifolia*
Field Maple, *Acer campestre*
Firethorn, *see* Pyracantha
Flame of the Forest (African Tulip Tree), *Spathodea campanulata* ⚠
Flax, *Linum* spp., *L. usitatissimum*
Fleabane, *see* Common Fleabane
Flowering Quince, *see* Japanese Quince
Forget-me-not, *Myosotis sylvatica*
Forsythia, *Forsythia* spp. ☻
French Bean, *see* Green Bean
Frogbit, *Hydrocharis morsus-ranae*

G

Gallberry (Inkberry), *Ilex glabra*
Garden Anchusa (Italian Bugloss), *Anchusa azurea* ☻
Garden Mignonette, *see* Sweet Mignonette
Garlic, *Allium sativum* ☻
Geranium (hardy), *see* Cranesbill
Germander, *Teucrium* x *lucidrys*
Giant Onion, *Allium giganteum*
Globe Artichoke (Cardoon), *Cynara cardunculus* (Scolymus Group)
Globe Flower (Blue Hedgehog), *Echinops ritro, E. bannaticus* ☻
Goat (Pussy) Willow, *Salix caprea* ☻
Godetia, Dwarf (Farewell to Spring), *Clarkia amoena* ☻
Golden Rain Tree (Pride of India), *Koelreuteria paniculata*
Goldenrod, *Solidago* spp. ☻

Gorse, *Ulex europaeus*
Grape, *Vitis vinifera*
Grape Hyacinth, *Muscari* spp. ☮
Green Bean (Climbing Bean, French Bean), *Phaseolus vulgaris* ☮
Gum Tree, *see* Eucalyptus
Gypsophila (Baby's Breath), *Gypsophila* spp. ☮

H, I

Hawthorn, *Crataegus* spp. (Single flower forms only) ☮
Hazel, *Corylus avellana*
Heather, *Erica carnea* (Alpine Heath) ☮, *E. cinerea* (Bell Heather)
  ☮, *Calluna vulgaris* (Ling) ☮
Hebe, *Hebe* spp. ☮
Heliconia (Lobster Claws), *Heliconia rostrata* ⚠
Hellebore (Christmas/Lenten Rose), *Helleborus* spp. ☮
Helenium (Sneezeweed), *Helenium* spp. ☮
Henbane, *Hyoscyamus niger* ⚠
Heuchera, *Heuchera* spp. ☮
Hoheria, *Hoheria* spp. ☮
Hollyhock, *Alcea rosea* ☮
Honesty, *Lunaria annua*
Horse Chestnut, *Aesculus hippocastanum*
Hosta, *Hosta* spp. ☮
Hyacinth, *Hyacinthus orientalis* ☮
Hydrangea, Climbing, *Hydrangea anomala* subsp. *petiolaris*
Hyssop, *Hyssopus officinalis*
Indian Bean Tree, *Catalpa bignonioides*
Indian Horse Chestnut, *Aesculus indica*
Inkberry, *see* Gallberry
Italian Bugloss, *see* Garden Anchusa
Ivy, *Hedera helix* ☮, *H. colchica* 'Dentata Variegata'
  (Persian Ivy)

J, K

Jacob's Ladder, *Polemonium caeruleum* ☯

Japanese Anemone, *Anemone hupehensis* var. *japonica* ☯

Japanese Angelica Tree, *Aralia elata*

Japanese Pagoda Tree, *Styphnolobium japonicum*

Japanese Aralia, *see* Fatsia Japonica

Japanese Rose, *Rosa rugosa* ☯

Japanese Wisteria, *Wisteria floribunda*

Joe Pye Weed, *Eupatorium maculatum*, *E. purpureum*

Japanese Quince (Flowering Quince), *Chaenomeles speciosa* ☯,
  C. japonica ☯

Jerusalem Artichoke, *Helianthus tuberosus*

Judas Tree, *Cercis siliquastrum*

Karaka, *see* New Zealand Laurel

Kingcup, *see* Marsh Marigold

Kiwi Fruit, *Actinidia deliciosa*

Knapweed, *see* Common Knapweed

Kohlrabi, *Brassica oleracea* (Gongylodes Group) ☯

L

Lacecap Hydrangea, *Hydrangea macrophylla* ☯

Lady's Smock, *see* Cuckoo Flower

Lavender, *Lavandula* spp. ☯

Lawn Daisy, *see* Daisy

Lemon, *Citrus* x *limon*

Lemon Balm, *Melissa officinalis*

Lemon Verbena, *Aloysia citrodora*

Lenten Rose, *see* Hellebore

Leopard's Bane, *Doronicum orientale*

Liatris (Button Snakewort), *Liatris spicata* ☯

Lilac, *Syringa* spp. ☯

Lilac Sage (Whorled Clary), *Salvia verticillata* 'Purple Rain'

Lily of the Valley Bush, *Pieris japonica* ☻
Lime (Linden), *Tilia cordata*
Lobster Claws, *see* Heliconia
Loganberry, *Rubus* x *loganobaccus*
Lovage, *Levisticum officinale*
Lupin, *Lupinus* spp. ☻

M

Mahonia, *Mahonia* spp. ☻
Mallow, *Malva* spp. and *Lavatera* spp. ☻
Maple, *Acer* spp.
Marrow, *Cucurbita pepo* ☻
Marsh Mallow (Kingcup), *Althaea officinalis*
Marsh Marigold, *Caltha palustris*
Masterwort, *see* Astrantia
Meadow Cranesbill, *Geranium pratense*
Medlar, *Mespilus germanica*
Melon, *Cucumis melo* ☻
Mexican Fleabane, *Erigeron karvinskianus*
Mexican Orange, *Choisya* spp. ☻
Michaelmas Daisy, *see* Aster
Milkweed, *see* Swamp Milkweed
Mint, *Mentha* spp.
Mock Orange, *Philadelphus* spp. ☻
Motherwort, *Leonurus cardiaca*
Mountain Ash (Rowan), *Sorbus aucuparia* spp. ☻
  and other *Sorbus* spp. ☻
Mountain Laurel, *Kalmia latifolia* ▲
Mullein, *Verbascum* spp. ☻
Musk Rose, Rosa moschata
Myrtle, *Myrtus communis*

N, O

Nasturtium, *Tropaeolum majus* ☑ (This is an edible form
  of the species)
Nasturtium, Climbing, *Tropaeolum tuberosum, T. speciosum* ☑
New Zealand Laurel (Karaka), *Corynocarpus laevigatus* ⚠
Oak, *Quercus* spp. ☑
Okra, *Abelmoschus esculentus*
Old Man's Beard, *see* Traveller's Joy
Oleander, *Nerium oleander* ⚠
Onion, *Allium cepa* ☑
Orange, *Citrus sinensis* ☑
Orange Ball Tree, *Buddleja globosa*
Oregano (Wild Marjoram), *Origanum vulgare*
Ornamental Onion, *see* Allium
Ox-Eye Daisy, *Leucanthemum vulgare*

P, Q

Parsley, *Petroselinum crispum*
Parsnip, *Pastinaca sativa* ☑
Pasque Flower, *Pulsatilla vulgaris*
Passion Flower, *Passiflora caerulea, P. edulis, P. incarnata*
Peach, *Prunus persica* ☑
Pear, *Pyrus communis* ☑
Peas, *Pisum sativum* ☑
Peony, *Paeonia* spp. ☑
Persian Ivy, *Hedera colchica* 'Dentata Variegata'
Phlox, *Phlox paniculata* ☑
Pincushion Flower, *see* Scabious
Plum, *Prunus domestica* ☑
Poppy, *Papaver* spp., *P. rhoeas* (Common Poppy) ☑, *P. orientale*
  (Oriental Poppy) ☑, also *Eschscholzia californica* (Californian
  Poppy) and *Meconopsis cambrica* (Welsh Poppy)

Potentilla (Cinquefoil), *Potentilla* spp. ☻

Pot Marigold (Common Marigold), *Calendula officinalis* ☻

Pride of India, *see* Golden Rain Tree

Privet, *Ligustrum ovalifolium* ⚠

Pumpkin, *Cucurbita pepo* spp. ☻

Purple Coneflower, *Echinacea purpurea* ☻

Purple Giant Hyssop, *Agastache scrophulariifolia*

Purple Viper's Bugloss, *Echium plantagineum* ☻

Purslane, *Portulaca oleracea*

Pussy Willow, *see* Goat Willow

Pyracantha (Firethorn), *Pyracantha* spp. ☻

Quince, *Cydonia oblonga* ☻

R

Ragged Robin, *Lychnis flos-cuculi*

Raspberry, *Rubus idaeus* ☻

Redcurrant, *Ribes rubrum* ☻

Red Horse Chestnut, *Aesculus* x *carnea*

Rhododendron, *Rhododendron* spp. ⚠

Rock Cress, *Arabis* spp. ☻, *A. alpina* ☻

Rocket, *Eruca vesicaria*

Rock Rose, *Cistus* spp. ☻

Rose, *Rosa* spp. ☻, particularly native species such as *R. canina* (Dog Rose), *R. rubiginosa* (Sweet Briar, Eglantine), *R. spinosissima* (Burnet or Scottish Rose)

Rose, Climbing/Rambling, *Rosa* spp. ☻

Rose Acacia, *Robinia hispida*

Rosebay Willowherb, *Chamaenerion angustifolium*

Rosemary, *Rosmarinus officinalis* ☻

Rowan, *see* Mountain Ash

Runner Bean, *Phaseolus coccineus* ☻

Russian Sage, *Perovskia atriplicifolia*

Russian Vine, *Fallopia baldschuanica*

S

Sage (Common Sage), *Salvia officinalis*
Salvia, *Salvia spp.* ☻
Salvinia, *Salvinia minima, S. natans*
Scabious (Pincushion Flower), *Scabiosa* spp. ☻
  and *Knautia arvensis* (Field Scabious)
Schumann Abelia, *Abelia parvifolia*
Sea Holly, *Eryngium spp.* ☻
Sea Pink (Thrift), *Armeria maritima* ☻
Sedum, *see* Stonecrop
Selfheal, *Prunella vulgaris*
Serbian Bellflower, *Campanula poscharskyana*
Shasta Daisy, *Leucanthemum* x *superbum* ☻
Shrubby Germander, *see* Tree/Shrubby Germander
Siberian Squill, *Scilla siberica* ☻
Sicilian Honey Garlic, *Nectaroscordum siculum*
Silkweed, *see* Swamp Milkweed
Skimmia, *Skimmia japonica* ☻
Silver Lime, *Tilia tomentosa* and *T. tomentosa* 'Orbicularis' ⬖
Sloe, *see* Blackthorn
Small-leaved Lime, *Tilia cordata*
Snowberry, *Symphoricarpos* spp.
Sneezeweed, *see* Helenium
Snowdrop, *Galanthus nivalis* ☻
Solomon's Seal, *Polygonatum* x *hybridum*
Sowbread, *see* Cyclamen
Spear Thistle (Bull Thistle), *Cirsium vulgare*
Spotted Cranesbill, *Geranium maculatum*
St John's Wort, *Hypericum* spp. ☻
Stachyurus, *Stachyurus praecox*
Star of Bethlehem, *Ornithogalum dubium*
Starflower, *see* Borage

Stargazer Lily, *Lilium* 'Stargazer' ◭
Strawberry Tree, *Arbutus unedo* ◭
Stonecrop, *Hylotelephium* spp. ◑ and *Sedum* spp. ◑
Strawberry, *Fragaria* x *ananassa* ◑
Sumach, *Rhus* spp.
Summer Savory, *Satureja hortensis*
Sunflower, *Helianthus* spp. ◑ (Not double forms)
Swamp Milkweed (Milkweed, Silkweed), *Asclepias incarnata*
Sweet Alison, *see* Alyssum
Sweet Alyssum, *see* Alyssum
Sweet Box, *Sarcococca hookeriana* var. *digyna* ◑,
  S. hookeriana var. *humilis* (Dwarf Sweet Box)
Sweet Cicely, *Myrrhis odorata*
Sweet Marjoram, *Origanum majorana*
Sweet Mignonette (Garden Mignonette), *Reseda odorata*
Sweet Olive, *Osmanthus fragrans*
Sweet Pea, *Lathyrus* spp. ◑
Sweet Pepper, *see* Bell Pepper
Sweet Violet (Wood Violet), *Viola odorata*
Sweet William, *Dianthus barbatus* ◑
Sycamore, *Acer pseudoplatanus* ◑

T

Tansy, *see* Common Tansy
Teasel, *Dipsacus* spp.
Thistle, *see* Cardoon, Globe Thistle, Spear Thistle
Thrift, *see* Sea Pink
Thyme, *Thymus* spp. ◑
Tickseed, *see* Coreopsis
Tobacco Plant, *Nicotiana* spp.
Turnip, *Brassica rapa* ◑
Traveller's Joy (Old Man's Beard), *Clematis vitalba*
Tree/Shrubby Germander, *Teucrium fruticans*

Tree Peony, *Paeonia suffruticosa* spp. ☯
Trumpet Flower (Angel's Trumpet), *Brugmansia* spp. ⚠
Tulip Tree, *Liriodendron tulipifera*
Tufted Vetch, *Vicia cracca*

V

Verbena, *Verbena bonariensis* ☯ and other *Verbena* spp.
Veronica/Speedwell, *Veronica longifolia* ☯
  and other *Veronica* spp.
Viburnum, *Viburnum* spp. ☯
Violet Sage (Wood Sage), *Salvia* x *sylvestris* ☯
Violet Willow, *Salix daphnoides*
Vine Lilac, *Hardenbergia violacea*
Viper's Bugloss, *Echium vulgare* ☯
Virginia Creeper, *Parthenocissus quinquefolia*, *P. henryana*
  (Chinese Virginia Creeper)

W, Y, Z

Wallflower, *Erysimum* spp. ☯
Walnut, *Juglans regia* ☯
Watercress, *Rorippa nasturtium-aquaticum*
Wayfaring Tree, *Viburnum lantana*
Weeping Silver Lime, *Tilia tomentosa* 'Petiolaris' ⚠
Weigela, *Weigela* spp. ☯
Whitebeam, *Sorbus aria* ☯
White Clover, *Trifolium repens*
Whitecurrant, *Ribes rubrum* ☯
White Horehound, *Marrubium vulgare*
White Mulberry, *Morus alba*
Whorled Clary, *see* Lilac Sage
Wild Blackberry (Bramble), *Rubus fruticosus* ☯
Wild Marjoram, *see* Oregano

Willow, *Salix* spp.
Winter Aconite, *Eranthis hyemalis*
Winter Crocus, *Crocus* spp.
Winter Daphne, *Daphne odora, D. mezereum*
Winter-flowering Cherry, *Prunus x subhirtella 'Autumnalis'*
Winter Honeysuckle, *Lonicera fragrantissima*
Winter Jasmine, *Jasminum nudiflorum*
Winter Pansy, *viola* ssp.
Winter Savory, *Satureja montana*
Wisteria, *Wisteria floribunda* (Japanese Wisteria), *W. sinensis* (Chinese Wisteria)
Witch Hazel, *Hamamelis* spp.
Wolfberry, *Symphoricarpos occidentalis*
Wood Anemone, *Anemone nemorosa*
Wood Germander, *Teucrium scorodonia*
Wood Sage, *see* Violet Sage
Wood Violet, *see* Sweet Violet
Yarrow, *Achillea* spp. , *see also* Common Yarrow
Yellow Jessamine, *Gelsemium sempervirens*
Yoshino Cherry, *Prunus* x *yedoensis*
Zinnia, *Zinnia* spp.

ACKNOWLEDGEMENTS

This book grew out of a small *'Planting for Honeybees'* booklet that I wrote to give away to gardening groups and local beekeeping societies. Harriet Butt, a commissioning editor at Quadrille, spotted its potential as a proper book and she and her team have been a joy to work with throughout this project. Thank you all.

Another big thank you goes to Jennifer Latham. With an enquiring mind and an extraordinary capacity for detail, she is the best editor any author could have.

Two other people I'd like to thank are the garden designer Jane Finlay, for sharing her great research on roof garden plantings, and John Chapple, one of Britain's most respected beekeepers. John first raised the issue of the crisis in honeybee forage over twenty years ago. He's been our constant mentor from the beginning and an inspiration to the work of Bermondsey Street Bees.

ACKNOWLEDGEMENTS

ABOUT THE AUTHOR

A freelance writer for more than thirty years, Sarah Wyndham Lewis has covered topics ranging from public affairs to design and interiors.

Since 2007, she has run the sustainable beekeeping business Bermondsey Street Bees with her husband, Dale Gibson. They live in London and Suffolk, where Sarah's bee-friendly garden is an ongoing project. In London, they work with charities and businesses to plant honeybee forage in public spaces.

Allergic to insect stings, Sarah is an unlikely bee enthusiast, but living at close quarters with hives for many years, learning, writing and running raw honey tastings has made her a passionate communicator on behalf of this gentle, industrious insect.

BERMONDSEY STREET BEES

Publishing Director Sarah Lavelle
Editor Harriet Butt
Copyeditor Jennifer Latham
Designer Maeve Bargman
Illustrator James Weston Lewis
Production Director Vincent Smith
Production Controller Tom Moore

Published in 2018 by Quadrille,
an imprint of Hardie Grant Publishing

Quadrille
52–54 Southwark Street
London SE1 1UN
quadrille.com

Reprinted in 2018 (three times), 2019 (three times), 2020
10 9 8

ISBN 978 1 78713 146 0

Printed in China

FSC
www.fsc.org
MIX
Paper from
responsible sources
FSC® C020056